A journey round my room

Xavier de Maistre, Henry Attwell

A

JOURNEY ROUND MY ROOM

BY

XAVIER DE MAISTRE

TRANSLATED FROM THE FRENCH, WITH A
NOTICE OF THE AUTHOR'S LIFE

BY

H. A. Attwell

NEW YORK
PUBLISHED BY HURD AND HOUGHTON
Cambridge: Riverside Press
1871

RIVERSIDE, CAMBRIDGE:
PRINTED BY H. O. HOUGHTON AND COMPANY.

PREFACE.

———◆———

THE author of the "Voyage autour de ma Chambre" was the younger brother of Count Joseph de Maistre, a well-known writer upon political and philosophical subjects. Chambéry was the place of their birth, but their family was of French origin. Both brothers were officers in the Sardinian army; and when Savoy was conquered by the French, Xavier de Maistre sought an asylum in Saint Petersburg, where his brother resided in the capacity of envoy from the court of Sardinia. Xavier entered the Russian army, distinguished himself in the war against Persia, and attained the rank of major-general.

Our interest in the "Voyage" is heightened by our knowledge that it was actually written during De Maistre's forty-two days' arrest at Turin, referred to in the third chapter. He sent the manuscript, which he regarded as a mere playful effort of his imagination, for his brother's perusal. Joseph was pleased with the book; and Xavier, who had an almost filial affection for his brother, was soon afterwards agreeably surprised by receiving, in place of his manuscript, the "Voyage" in print.

This success encouraged him to begin a sequel to the "Voyage." Joseph, however, disapproved of this new attempt. The "Expédition Nocturne" was, notwithstanding, finished, and was published some years later.

Xavier de Maistre's next production (1811) was "Le Lépreux de la Cité d'Aoste," a very touching and gracefully written narrative. It occupies but a few pages ; and, as it is to be found in almost every good anthology of French literature, is perhaps the best known of our author's works.

His other books are "Les Prisonniers du Caucase" (1815) and "La Jeune Sibérienne," both of them charming works, containing faithful pictures of domestic scenes with which we are little familiar through other sources.

From his childhood Xavier de Maistre was devoted to painting. He deservedly gained considerable reputation as a painter of miniature portraits and landscapes.

Nor did he neglect science while devoting himself to art and literature. He applied himself so successfully to the study of chemistry that he was able to communicate several valuable " Mémoires " to the Academy of Turin, of which he was a member.

Xavier de Maistre died (1852) at an advanced age in his adopted country, where he had married, and which he only quitted once, for a brief season.

———◆———

Some apology for publishing this translation is perhaps necessary.

Although in France the " Voyage " retains the high esteem in which it has been held for half a century, it is hardly known in England, except by those who are familiar with the French language and literature.

During the last twenty years the propor-
tion of educated persons in this country
who are unable to enjoy a French book in
the original has greatly decreased. Still,
there are some to whom a translation of
this delightful work may be acceptable.

To them I offer the pleasant labor of a
few leisure hours ; but not without assuring
them that in endeavoring to reproduce
faithfully the author's ideas, I have felt at
every paragraph how true it is that "*le
style se traduit pas*," — "style is untrans-
latable.

The *headings* of the chapters are not
De Maistre's. They appear in Tardieu's
pretty little edition of the "Voyage." The
miniatures, by M. Veyssier, are from the
same source.

H. A.

CONTENTS.

b

Contents. xi

I.

A Book of Discoveries.

WHAT more glorious than to open for one's self a new career, — to appear suddenly before the learned world with a book of discoveries in one's hand, like an unlooked-for comet blazing in the empyrean!

No longer will I keep my book in obscurity. Behold it, gentlemen; read it! I have undertaken and performed a forty-two days' journey round my room. The interesting observations I have made, and the constant pleasure I have experienced all along the road, made me wish to publish my travels; the certainty of being useful decided the matter. And when I think of the number of unhappy ones to whom I offer a never failing resource for weary moments, and a balm for the ills they suffer, my heart is filled with inexpressible satisfaction. The pleasure to be found in travelling round one's room is sheltered from the restless jealousy of men, and is independent of Fortune.

Surely there is no being so miserable as to be without a retreat to which he can withdraw and hide himself from the world. Such a hiding-place will contain all the preparations our journey requires.

Every man of sense will, I am sure, adopt my system, whatever may be his peculiar character or temperament. Be he miserly or prodigal, rich or poor, young or old, born beneath the torrid zone or near the poles, he may travel with me. Among the immense family of men who throng the earth, there is not one, no, not one (I mean of those who inhabit rooms), who, after reading this book can refuse his approbation of the new mode of travelling I introduce into the world.

II.

Eulogy of the Journey.

I MIGHT fairly begin the eulogium of my
journey by saying it has cost me nothing. This point merits attention. It will
gain for it the praise and welcome of people
of moderate means. And not of these
only : there is another class with whom its
success will, on this account, be even more
certain. "And who are they ?" you ask.
Why, the rich, to be sure. And then,
again, what a comfort the new mode of travelling will be to the sick ; they need not
fear bleak winds or change of weather.
And what a thing, too, it will be for cowards ; they will be safe from pitfalls or
quagmires. Thousands who hitherto did
not dare, others who were not able, and

others to whom it never occurred to think of such a thing as going on a journey, will make up their minds to follow my example. Surely, the idlest person will not hesitate to set out with me on a pleasure jaunt which will cost him neither trouble nor money. Come then, let us start! Follow me, all ye whom the "pangs of despised love" or the slights of friends keep within doors, — follow me far from the meannesses and unkindnesses of men. Be ye unhappy, sick, or weary, follow me. Ye idle ones, arouse ye, one and all. And ye who brood over gloomy projects of reform and retreat, on account of some infidelity, — amiable anchorites of an evening's duration, who renounce the world for your boudoir, — come, and be led by me to banish these dark thoughts; you lose a moment's pleasure without gaining a moment's wisdom! Deign to accompany me on my journey. We will jog cheerfully and by easy stages along the road of travellers who have seen both Rome and Paris. No obstacle shall hinder our way ; and giving ourselves up gaily to Imagination, we will follow her whithersoever it may be her good pleasure to lead us.

III.

Laws and Customs.

HOW many inquisitive people there are in the world! I am sure my reader wants to know why the journey round my room has lasted forty-two days rather than forty-three, or any other number. But how am I to tell him what I do not know myself? All I can say is, that if the work is too long for him, it is not my fault that it was not shorter. I dismiss all the pride a traveller may fairly indulge in, and candidly declare I should have been well contented, for my part, with a single chapter. It is quite true that I made myself as comfortable as possible in my room; but still, alas, I was not my own master in the matter of leaving it. Nay, more, I even think that had it not been for the intervention of certain powerful persons who interested themselves in me, and towards whom I entertain a lively sense of gratitude, I should have had ample time for producing a folio volume ; so prejudiced in my favor were the guardians who made me travel round my room.

And yet, intelligent reader, see how wrong these men were ; and understand clearly, if you can, the argument I am about to put before you.

Can there be anything more natural or more just than to draw your sword upon a man who happens to tread on your toe, who lets slip a bitter word during a moment's vexation caused by your own thoughtlessness, or who has had the misfortune to gain favor in the sight of your lady-love ?

Under such or like circumstances, you betake yourself to a meadow, and there, like Nicole and the " Bourgeois Gentilhomme," you try to give the fourth cut while your adversary parries tierce ; and, that vengeance may be fully satisfied, you present your naked breast to him, thus running the risk of being killed by your enemy, in order to be avenged.

It is evident that such a custom is most reasonable. And yet, we sometimes meet with people who disapprove of so praiseworthy a course. But what is about of a piece with the rest of the business is, that the very persons who condemn the course we have described, and who would have it regarded as a grave error, would judge still more harshly any one who refused to commit it. More than one unlucky wight has, by endeavoring to conform to their opinion, lost his reputation and his livelihood. So that, when people are so unfortunate as to have an affair of honor to settle, it would not be a bad plan to cast lots to see whether it shall be arranged according to law, or according to fashion. And as law and fashion are at variance, the judges might decide upon their sentence by the aid of dice, — and probably it is to some such decision as this that we should have to refer in order to explain how it came about that my journey lasted just two and forty days.

IV.

Latitude and Topography.

MY room is situated in latitude 48°
east, according to the measurement
of Father Beccaria. It lies east and west,
and, if you keep very close to the wall,
forms a parallelogram of thirty-six steps
round. My journey will, however, be
longer than this; for I shall traverse my
room up and down and across, without rule
or plan. I shall even zig-zag about, following, if needs be, every possible geometrical
line. I am no admirer of people who are
such masters of their every step and every
idea that they can say : "To-morrow I shall
make three calls, write four letters, and
finish this or that work." So open is my
soul to all sorts of ideas, tastes, and feel-

ings; so greedily does it absorb whatever
comes first, that . . . . but why should
it deny itself the delights that are scattered
along life's hard path ?   So few and far between are they, that it would indeed be
senseless not to stop, and even turn aside,
to gather such as are placed within our
reach.   Of these joys, none, to my thinking, is more attractive than following the
course of one's fancies as a hunter follows
his game, without pretending to keep to
any set route.   Hence, when I travel in
my room, I seldom keep to a straight line.
From my table I go towards a picture
which is placed in a corner; thence I set
out in an oblique direction for the door;
and then, although on starting I had intended to return to my table, yet, if I
chance to fall in with my arm-chair on the
way, I at once, and most unceremoniously,
take up my quarters therein.   By the by,
what a capital article of furniture an arm-

chair is, and, above all, how convenient to a thoughtful man. In long winter evenings it is ofttimes sweet, and always prudent, to stretch yourself therein, far from the bustle of crowded assemblies. A good fire, some books and pens; what safeguards these against *ennui!* And how pleasant, again, to forget books and pens in order to stir the fire, while giving one's self up to some agreeable meditation, or stringing together a few rhymes for the amusement of friends, as the hours glide by and fall into eternity, without making their sad passage felt.

V.

The Bed.

NEXT to my arm-chair, as we go northward, my bed comes into sight. It is placed at the end of my room, and forms the most agreeable perspective. It is very pleasantly situated, and the earliest rays of the sun play upon my curtains. On fine summer days I see them come creeping, as the sun rises, all along the whitened wall. The elm-trees opposite my windows divide them into a thousand patterns as they dance upon my bed, and, reflecting its rose-and-white color, shed a charming tint around. I hear the confused twitter of the swallows that have taken possession of my roof, and the warbling of the birds that people the elms.

Then do a thousand smiling fancies fill my soul ; and in the whole universe no being enjoys an awakening so delightful, so peaceful, as mine.

I confess that I do indeed revel in these sweet moments, and prolong as far as I can the pleasure it gives me to meditate in the comfortable warmth of my bed. What scene can adapt itself so well to the imagination, and awaken such delicious ideas, as the couch on which my fancy floats me into the forgetfulness of self! Here it is that the mother, intoxicated with joy at the birth of a son, forgets her pangs. Hither it is that fantastic pleasures, the fruit of fancy or of hope, come to agitate us. In a word, it is here that during one half of a life-time we forget the annoyances of the other half.

But what a host of thoughts, some agreeable, some sad, throng my brain at once, — strange minglings of terrible and delicious pictures !

A bed sees us born, and sees us die. It is the ever changing scene upon which the human race play by turns interesting dramas, laughable farces, and fearful tragedies. It is a cradle decked with flowers. A throne of love. A sepulchre.

VI.

For Metaphysicians.

THIS chapter is for metaphysicians, and for metaphysicians only. It will throw a great light upon man's nature. It is the prism with which to analyze and decompose the human faculties, by separating the animal force from the pure rays of intellect.

It would be impossible for me to explain how I came to burn my fingers at the very onset of my journey without expounding to my reader my system of the *Soul and the Animal.* [1] And besides, this metaphysical discovery has so great an influ-

---

[1] *Bête* is not translatable here. The English word *animal* is hardly nearer than *beast.* *Bête* is a milder word than *beast,* and when used metaphorically, implies silliness rather than brutality. In some cases our *creature* would translate it, *Pauvre bête ! Poor creature !*

2

ence on my thoughts and actions, that it would be very difficult to understand this book if I did not begin by giving the key to its meaning.

Various observations have enabled me to perceive that man is made up of a soul and an animal. These two beings are quite distinct, but they are so dovetailed one into the other, or upon the other, that the soul must, if we would make the distinction between them, possess a certain superiority over the animal.

I have it from an old professor (and this is as long ago as I can remember), that Plato used to call matter the OTHER. This is all very well; but I prefer giving this name *par excellence* to the animal which is joined to our soul. This substance it is which is really the OTHER, and which plays such strange tricks upon us. It is easy enough to see, in a sort of general way, that man is twofold. But this, they say, is

because he is made up of soul and body;
and they accuse the body of I don't know
how many things, and very inconsistently,
seeing that it can neither feel nor think.
It is upon the animal that the blame should
fall; upon that sensitive being, which,
while it is perfectly distinct from the soul,
is a real individual, enjoying a separate
existence, with its own tastes, inclinations,
and will, and which only ranks higher than
other animals, because it is better educated
than they, and is provided with more perfect organs.

Ladies and gentlemen! Be as proud of
your intellect as you please, but be very
suspicious of the OTHER, especially when
you are together.

I have experimented I know not how oft,
upon the union of these two heterogeneous
creatures. I have, for instance, clearly as-
certained that the soul can make herself
obeyed by the animal, and that, by way of

retaliation, the animal makes the soul act contrary to its own inclination. The one, as a rule, has the legislative, the other the executive power, but these two are often at variance. The great business of a man of genius is to train his animal well, in order that it may go alone, while the soul, delivered from this troublesome companion, can raise herself to the skies.

But this requires illustration. When, sir, you are reading a book, and an agreeable idea suddenly enters your imagination, your soul attaches herself to the new idea at once, and forgets the book, while your eyes follow mechanically the words and lines. You get through the page without understanding it, and without remembering what you have read. Now this is because your soul, having ordered her companion to read to her, gave no warning of the short absence she contemplated, so that the OTHER went on reading what the soul no longer attended to.

VII.

The Soul.

IS not this clear to you ? Let us illustrate it still farther.

One day last summer at an appointed hour, I was wending my way to court. I had been sketching all day, and my soul, choosing to meditate upon painting, left the duty of taking me to the king's palace to the animal.

How sublime, thought my soul, is the painter's art ! Happy is he who is touched by the aspect of nature, and does not depend upon his pictures for a livelihood ; who does not paint solely as a pastime, but struck with the majesty of a beautiful form, and the wonderful way in which the light with its thousand tints plays upon the

human face, strives to imitate in his works
the wonderful effects of nature! Happy,
too, is the painter who is led by love of
landscape into solitary paths, and who can
make his canvas breathe the feeling of sadness with which he is inspired by a gloomy
wood or a desert plain. His productions
imitate and reproduce nature. He creates
new seas and dark caverns into which the
sun has never peered. At his command,
coppices of evergreens spring into life, and
the blue of heaven is reflected on his pictures. He darkens the air, and we hear the
roar of the storm. At another time he
presents to the eye of the wondering beholder the delightful plains of ancient Sici-
ly : startled nymphs flee the pursuit of a
satyr through the bending reeds ; temples
of stately architecture raise their grand
fronts above the sacred forest that sur-
rounds them. Imagination loses itself
among the still paths of this ideal country.

Bluish backgrounds blend with the sky, and the whole landscape, reproduced in the waters of a tranquil river, forms a scene that no tongue can describe.

While my soul was thus reflecting, the *other* went its way, Heaven knows whither! Instead of going to court, according to orders, it took such a turn to the left, that my soul just caught it up at Madame de Hautcastel's door, full half a mile from the Palais Royal!

Now I leave the reader to fancy what might have been the consequence had the truant visited so beautiful a lady alone.

VIII.

The Animal.

IF it is both useful and agreeable to have a soul so disengaged from matter that we can let it travel alone whenever we please, this has also its disadvantages. Through this, for instance, I got the burn I spoke of a few chapters back.

I generally leave my animal to prepare my breakfast. Its care it is to slice and toast my bread. My coffee it makes admirably, and helps itself thereto without my soul's concerning herself in the transaction. But this is a very rare and nice performance to execute ; for though it is easy enough while busied in a mechanical operation, to think of something quite different, it is extremely difficult, so to speak, to watch one's self-work, or, if I express myself systematically, to employ one's soul to examine the animal's progress, and to watch its work without taking part in it. This is the most extraordinary metaphysical feat a man can execute.

I had rested my tongs on the embers to toast my bread, and some little time afterwards, while my soul was travelling, a burning stick fell on the hearth : my poor animal seized the tongs, and I burnt my fingers.

IX.

Philosophy.

I HOPE I have sufficiently developed my ideas in the foregoing chapters to furnish you, good reader, with matter for thought, and to enable you to make discoveries along the brilliant career before you. You cannot be other than highly satisfied with yourself if you succeed in the long run in making your soul travel alone. The pleasure afforded by this power will amply counterbalance any inconvenience that may arise from it. What more flattering delight is there than the being able thus to expand one's existence, to occupy at once earth and heaven, to double, so to speak, one's being? Is it not man's eternal, insatiable desire to augment his strength and his faculties, to be where he is not, to recall the past, and live in the future? He would fain command armies, preside over learned societies, and be the idol of the fair. And, if he attain to all this, then he regrets the tranquillity of a rural life, and envies the shepherd's cot. His plans, his hopes, are constantly foiled by the ills that flesh is heir to. He can find happiness nowhere. A quarter of an hour's journey with me will show him the way to it.

Ah, why does he not leave to the OTHER those carking cares and that tormenting ambition. Come, my poor friend! Make but an effort to burst from thy prison, and from the height of heaven, whither I am about to lead thee, from the midst of the celestial shades, from the empyrean itself, behold thy *animal* run along the road to fortune and honor. See with what gravity it walks among men. The crowd falls back with respect, and believe me, none will remark that it is alone. The people among whom it walks care very little whether it has a soul or not, whether it thinks or not. A thousand sentimental women will fall desperately in love with it without discovering the defect. It may even raise itself without thy soul's help to the highest favor and fortune. Nay, I should not be astonished if, on thy return from the empyrean, thy soul, on getting home, were to find itself in the *animal* of a noble lord.

X.

The Portrait.

BUT you must not let yourself think
that instead of keeping my promise
to describe my journey round my room, I
am beating the bush to see how I can
evade the difficulty. This would be a
great mistake on your part. For our journey is really going on; and while my soul,
falling back on her own resources, was in
the last chapter threading the mazy paths
of metaphysics, I had so placed myself in
my arm-chair, that its front legs being
raised about two inches from the floor, I
was able, by balancing myself from left to
right, to make way by degrees, and at last,
almost without knowing it, to get close to
the wall, for this is how I travel when not

pressed for time. When there, my hand possessed itself by a mere mechanical effort, of the portrait of Madame de Haut-castel ; and the OTHER amused itself with removing the dust which covered it. This occupation produced a feeling of quiet pleasure, and the pleasure was conveyed to my soul, lost though it was in the vast plains of heaven. For it is well to observe that when the mind is thus travelling in space, it still keeps linked to the senses by a secret and subtle chain ; so that, without being distracted from its occupations, it can participate in the peaceful joys of the OTHER. But should this pleasure reach a certain pitch, or should the soul be struck by some unexpected vision, it forthwith descends swift as lightning, and resumes its place.

And that is just what happened to me while dusting the picture. Whilst the cloth removed the dust, and brought to

light those flaxen curls and the wreaths of
roses that crowned them, my soul, from the
sun, whither she had transported herself,
felt a slight thrill of pleasure, and partook
sympathetically of the joy of my heart.
This joy became less indistinct and more
lively, when, by a single sweep, the beautiful forehead of that. charming face was
revealed. My soul was on the point of
leaving the skies in order to enjoy the spectacle. But had she been in the Elysian
Fields, had she been engaged in a seraphic
concert, she could not have stayed a single
second longer when her companion, glow-
ing with the work, seized a proffered
sponge, and passed it at once over the eye-
brows and the eyes, over the nose, over
that mouth, ah heavens ! — my heart beats
at the thought — over the chin and neck !
It was the work of an instant. The whole
face .seemed suddenly recalled into existence. My soul precipitated herself like a

falling star from the sky. She found the
OTHER in a state of ecstasy, which she herself increased by sharing it. This strange
and unexpected position caused all thought
of time and space to vanish from my mind.
I lived for a moment in the past, and, contrary to the order of nature, I grew young
again. Yes, before me stands that adored
one ; 'tis she, her very self! She smiles
on me, she will speak and own her love.
That glance! . . . . come, let me press
thee to my heart, O, my loved one, my other
self! Partake with me this intoxicating
bliss! The moment was short, but ravishing. Cool reason soon reasserted her sway,
and in the twinkling of an eye I had grown a
whole year older. My heart grew icy cold,
and I found myself on a level with the
crowd of heedless ones who throng the
earth.

XI.

Rose and White.

BUT we must not anticipate events. My hurry to communicate to the reader my system of the soul and animal caused me to abandon the description of my bed earlier than I ought to have done. When I have completed this description, I will continue my journey where I interrupted it in the last chapter. But let me pray you to bear in mind that we left one half of my *ego* four steps from my bureau, close to the wall, and holding the portrait of Madame de Hautcastel.

In speaking of my bed, I forgot to recommend every man to have, if possible, a bed with rose and white furniture. There can be no doubt that colors so far affect us as to make us cheerful or sad, according to their hues. Now, rose and white are two colors that are consecrated to pleasure. Nature in bestowing them upon the rose has given her the crown of Flora's realm. And when the sky would announce to the world a fine day, it paints the clouds at sunrise with this charming tint.

One day we were with some difficulty climbing a steep pathway. The amiable Rosalie, whose agility had given her wings, was far in front. We could not overtake her. All on a sudden, having reached the top of a hillock, she turned toward us to take breath, and smiled at our slowness. Never, perhaps, did the two colors whose praise I proclaim so triumph. Her burning cheeks, her coral lips, her alabaster neck, were thrown into relief by the verdure around, and entranced us all. We could not but pause and gaze upon her. I will not speak of her blue eyes, or of the glance she cast upon us, because this would be go-ing from the subject, and because I dwell upon these memories as little as possible. Let it suffice that I have given the best illustration conceivable of the superiority of these two colors over all others, and of their influence upon the happiness of man.

Here will I stop for to-day. Of what subject can I treat which would not now be insipid? What idea is not effaced by *this* idea? I do not even know when I shall be able to resume my work. If I go on with it at all, and if the reader desire to see its termination, let him betake himself to the angel who distributes thoughts, and beg him to cease to mingle with the discon-nected thoughts he showers upon me at every moment the image of that hillock.

If this precaution is not taken, my jour-ney will be a failure.

XII.

The Hillock.

VEYSSIER D.   GUILLAUME S.

XIII.

A Halt.

MY efforts are useless. I must sojourn here awhile, whether I will or not. The " Halt !" is irresistible.

XIV.

Joannetti.

I REMARKED that I was singularly
fond of meditating when influenced by
the agreeable warmth of my bed ; and that
its agreeable color added not a little to the
pleasure I experienced.

That I may be provided with this enjoyment, my servant is directed to enter
my room half an hour before my time for
rising. I hear him moving about my room
with a light step, and stealthily managing
his preparations. This noise just suffices
to convey to me the pleasant knowledge
that I am slumbering, — a delicate pleasure
this, unknown to most men. You are just
awake enough to know you are not entirely
so, and to make a dreamy calculation that

the hour for business and worry is still in the sand-glass of time. Gradually my man grows noisier; it is so hard for him to restrain himself, and he knows too that the fatal hour draws near. He looks at my watch, and jingles the seals as a warning. But I turn a deaf ear to him. There is no imaginable cheat I do not put upon the poor fellow to lengthen the blissful moment. I give him a hundred preliminary orders. He knows that these orders, given somewhat peevishly, are mere excuses for my staying in bed without seeming to wish to do so. But this he affects not to see through, and I am truly thankful to him.

At last, when I have exhausted all my resources, he advances to the middle of the room, and with folded arms, plants himself there in a perfectly immovable position. It must be admitted that it would be impossible to show disapproval of my idleness with greater judgment and address. I never resist this tacit invitation, but, stretching out my arms to show I understand him, get up at once.

If the reader will reflect upon the behavior of my servant, he will convince himself that in certain delicate matters of this kind, simplicity and good sense are much better than the sharpest wit. I dare assert that the most studied discourse on the impropriety of sloth would not make me spring so readily from my bed as the silent reproach of Monsieur Joannetti.

This Monsieur Joannetti is a thoroughly honest fellow, and at the same time just the man for such a traveller as I. He is accustomed to the frequent journeys of my soul, and never laughs at the inconsistencies of the OTHER. He even directs it occasionally when it is alone, so that one might say it is then conducted by two souls. When it is dressing, for instance, he will warn it by a gesture that it is on the point of putting on its stockings the wrong way, or its coat before its waistcoat.

Many a time has my soul been amused at seeing poor Joannetti running after this foolish creature under the arches of the citadel, to remind it of a forgotten hat or handkerchief. One day, I must confess, had it not been for this faithful servant, who caught it up just at the bottom of the staircase, the silly creature would have presented itself at court without a sword, as boldly as if it had been the chief gentleman-usher, bearing the august rod.

XV.

A Difficulty.

"COME, Joannetti," I said, "hang up this picture." He had helped to clean it, and had no more notion than the man in the moon what had produced our chapter on the portrait. He it was, who, of his own accord, held out the wet sponge, and who, through that seemingly unimportant act, caused my soul to travel a hundred millions of leagues in a moment of time. Instead of restoring it to its place, he held it to examine it in his turn. A difficulty, a problem, gave him an inquisitive air, which I did not fail to observe.

"Well, and what fault do you find with that portrait?" said I.

"O, none at all, sir."

"But come now, you have some remark to make, I know."

He placed it upright on one of the wings of my bureau, and then drawing back a little, "I wish, sir," he said, "that you would explain how it is that in whatever part of the room one may be, this portrait always watches you. In the morning, when I am making your bed, the face turns towards me; and if I move toward the window, it still looks at me, and follows me with its eyes as I go about."

"So that, Joannetti," said I, "if my room were full of people, that beautiful lady would eye every one, on all sides, at once."

"Just so, sir."

"She would smile on every comer and goer, just as she would on me?"

Joannetti gave no further answer. I stretched myself in my easy-chair, and, hanging down my head, gave myself up to the most serious meditations. What a ray of light fell upon me! Alack, poor lover! While thou pinest away, far from thy mistress, at whose side another perhaps, has already replaced thee ; whilst thou fixest thy longing eyes on her portrait, imagining that at least in picture, thou art the sole being she deigns to regard, — the perfidious image, as faithless as the original, bestows its glances on all around, and smiles on every one alike !

And in this behold a moral resemblance between certain portraits and their originals, which no philosopher, no painter, no observer, had before remarked.

I go on from discovery to discovery.

VESSIER   GUILLAUME.

XVI.

Solution.

JOANNETTI remained in the attitude I
have described, awaiting the explanation
he had asked of me. I withdrew my head
from the folds of my travelling dress, into
which I had thrust it that I might meditate
more at my ease; and after a moment's
silence, to enable me to collect my thoughts
after the reflections I had just made, I said,
turning my arm-chair toward him, —

"Do you not see that as a picture is a
plane surface, the rays of light proceeding
from each point on that surface. . . . ?"

At that explanation, Joannetti stretched

his eyes to their very widest, while he kept his mouth half open. These two movements of the human face express, according to the famous Le Brun, the highest pitch of astonishment. It was, without doubt, my *animal*, that had undertaken this dissertation, while my soul was well aware that Joannetti knew nothing whatever about plane surfaces and rays of light. The prodigious dilatation of his eyelids caused me to draw back. I ensconced my head in the collar of my travelling coat, and this so effectively that I well-nigh succeeded in altogether hiding it. I determined to dine where I was. The morning was far advanced, and another step in my room would have delayed my dinner until night-fall. I let myself slip to the edge of my chair, and putting both feet on the mantel-piece, patiently awaited my meal. This was a most comfortable attitude; indeed, it would be difficult to find another possessing so many advantages, and so well adapted to the inevitable sojourns of a long voyage.

At such moments, Rose, my faithful dog, never fails to come and pull at the skirts of my travelling dress that I may take her up. She finds a very convenient ready-made bed at the angle formed by the two parts of my body. A V admirably represents my position. Rose jumps to her post if I do not take her up quickly enough to please her, and I often find her there without knowing how she has come. My hands fall into a position which minister to her well-being, and this, either through a sympathy existing between this good-natured creature and myself, or through the merest chance. But no, I do not believe in that miserable doctrine of *chance*, — in that unmeaning word! I would rather believe in animal magnetism.

There is such reality in the relations which exist between these two animals,

that when out of sheer distraction, I put
my two feet on the mantel-piece and have
no thought at all about a *halt*, dinner-time
not being near, Rose, observing this movement, shows by a slight wag of her tail the
pleasure she enjoys.   Reserve keeps her in
her place.   The *other* perceives this and is
gratified by it, though quite unable to reason upon its cause.   And thus a mute dialogue is established between them, a pleasing interchange of sensations which could
not be attributed to simple chance.

XVII.

Rose.

DO not reproach me for the prolixity with which I narrate the details of my journey. This is the wont of travellers. When one sets out for the ascent of Mont Blanc, or to visit the yawning tomb of Empedocles, the minutest particulars are carefully described. The number of persons who formed the party, the number of mules, the quality of the food, the excellent appetite of the travellers, — everything, to the very stumbling of the quadrupeds, is carefully noted down for the instruction of the sedentary world.

Upon this principle, I resolved to speak of my dog Rose, — an amiable creature for

4

whom I entertain sincere regard, — and to devote a whole chapter to her.

We have lived together for six years, and there has never been any coolness between us, and if ever any little disputes have arisen, the fault has been chiefly on my side, and Rose has always made the first advances towards reconciliation.

In the evening, if she has been scolded she withdraws sadly and without a murmur. The next morning at daybreak, she stands near my bed in a respectful attitude, and at her master's slightest movement, at the first sign of his being awake, she makes her presence known by rapidly tapping my little table with her tail.

And why should I refuse my affection to this good-natured creature that has never ceased to love me ever since we have lived together? My memory would not enable me to enumerate all the people who have interested themselves in me but to forget me. I have had some few friends, several lady-loves, a host of acquaintances; and now I am to all these people as if I had never lived; they have forgotten my very name.

And yet what protestations they made, what offers of assistance! Their purse was at my disposal, and they begged me to depend upon their eternal and entire friendship!

Poor Rose, who has made me no promises, renders me the greatest service that can be bestowed upon humanity, for she has always loved her master, and loves him still. And this is why I do not hesitate to say that she shares with my other friends the affection I feel towards them.

XVIII.

Reserve.

WE left Joannetti standing motionless before me, in an attitude of astonishment, awaiting the conclusion of the sublime explanation I had begun.

When he saw me bury my head in my dressing-gown, and thus end my dissertation, he did not doubt for a moment that I had stopped short for lack of resources, and that he had fairly overcome me by the knotty question he had plied me with.

Notwithstanding the superiority he had hereby gained over me, he felt no movement of pride, and did not seek to profit by his advantage. After a moment's silence, he took the picture, put it back in its place, and withdrew softly on tip-toe. He felt that his presence was a sort of humiliation to me, and his delicacy of feeling led him thus to retire unobserved. His behavior on this occasion interested me greatly, and gave him a higher place than ever in my affections. And he will have too, without doubt, a place in the heart of my readers. If there be one among them who will refuse it him after reading the next chapter, such a one must surely have a heart of stone.

XIX.

A Tear.

"GOOD Heavens!" said I to him one day, "three times have I told you to buy me a brush. What a head the fellow has!" He answered not a word; nor had he the evening before made any reply to a like expostulation. "This is very odd," I thought to myself, "he is generally so very particular."

"Well, go and get a duster to wipe my shoes with," I said angrily. While he was on his way, I regretted that I had spoken so sharply, and my anger entirely subsided when I saw how carefully he tried to remove the dust from my shoes without touching my stockings. "What," I said to myself, "are there then men who brush others' shoes for *money!*" This word *money* came upon me like a flash of lightning. I suddenly remembered that for a long time my servant had not had any money from me.

"Joannetti," said I, drawing away my foot, "have you any change?"

A smile of justification lit up his face at the question.

"No, sir; for the last week I have not possessed a penny. I have spent all I had for your little purchases."

"And the brush? I suppose that is why · . . . . ?"

He still smiled. Now, he might very well have said, "No, sir; I am not the empty-headed ass you would make out your faithful servant to be. Pay me the one pound two shillings and sixpence halfpenny you owe me, and then I'll buy you your brush." But no, he bore this ill treatment rather than cause his master to blush at his unjust anger.   And may Heaven bless him !   Philosophers, Christians ! have you read this ?

" Come, Joannetti," said I, " buy me the brush."

" But, sir, will you go like that, with one shoe clean, and the other dirty ? "

" Go, go !" I replied, " never mind about the dust, never mind that."

He went out. I took the duster, and daintily wiped my left shoe, on which a tear of repentance had fallen.

XX.

Albert and Charlotte.

THE walls of my room are hung with engravings and pictures, which adorn it greatly. I should much like to submit them to the reader's inspection, that they might amuse him along the road we have to traverse before we reach my bureau. But it is as impossible to describe a picture well, as to paint one from a description.

What an emotion he would feel in contemplating the first drawing that presents itself! He would see the unhappy Charlotte,[1] slowly, and with a trembling hand, wiping Albert's pistols. Dark forebodings, and all the agony of hopeless, inconsolable love, are imprinted on her features, while

[1] Vide *Werther*, chapter xxviii.

the cold-hearted Albert, surrounded by bags of law papers and various old documents, turns with an air of indifference towards his friend to bid him good-by. Many a time have I been tempted to break the glass that covers this engraving, that I might tear Albert away from the table, rend him to pieces, and trample him under foot. But this would not do away with the Alberts. There will always be sadly too many of them in the world. What sensitive man is there who has not such a one near him, who receives the overflowings of his soul, the gentle emotions of his heart, and the flights of his imagination just as the rock receives the waves of the sea? Happy is he who finds a friend whose heart and mind harmonize with his own ; a friend who adheres to him by likeness of tastes, feeling, and knowledge ; a friend who is not the prey of ambition or greediness, who prefers the shade of a tree to the pomp of a court ! Happy is he who has a friend !

XXI.

A Friend.

I HAD a friend. Death took him from
me. He was snatched away at the beginning of his career, at the moment when
his friendship had become a pressing need
to my heart. We supported one another
in the hard toil of war. We had but one
pipe between us. We drank out of the
same cup. We slept beneath the same
tent. And, amid our sad trials, the spot
where we lived together became to us a
new father-land. I had seen him exposed
to all the perils of a disastrous war. Death
seemed to spare us to each other. His

deadly missives were exhausted around my friend a thousand times over without reaching him ; but this was but to make his loss more painful to me. The tumult of war, and the enthusiasm which possesses the soul at the sight of danger might have prevented his sighs from piercing my heart, while his death would have been useful to his country, and damaging to the enemy. Had he died thus, I should have mourned him less.   But to lose him amid the joys of our winter-quarters ; to see him die at the moment when he seemed full of health, and when our intimacy was rendered closer by rest and tranquillity, — ah, this was a blow from which I can never recover !

But his memory lives in my heart, and there alone.   He is forgotten by those who surrounded him, and who have replaced him.   And this makes his loss the more sad to me.

Nature, in like manner indifferent to the

fate of individuals, dons her green spring robe, and decks herself in all her beauty near the cemetery where he rests. The trees cover themselves with foliage, and intertwine their branches ; the birds warble under the leafy sprays ; the insects hum among the blossoms : everything breathes joy in this abode of death.

And in the evening, when the moon shines in the sky, and I am meditating in this sad place, I hear the grasshopper, hidden in the grass that covers the silent grave of my friend, merrily pursuing his unwearied song. The unobserved destruction of human beings, as well as all their misfortunes, are counted for nothing in the grand total of events.

The death of an affectionate man who breathes his last surrounded by his afflicted friends, and that of a butterfly killed in a flower's cup by the chill air of morning, are but two similar epochs in the course of nature. Man is but a phantom, a shadow, a mere vapor that melts into the air.

But day-break begins to whiten the sky. The gloomy thoughts that troubled me vanish with the darkness, and hope awakens again in my heart. No! He who thus suffuses the east with light, has not made it to shine upon my eyes only to plunge me into the night of annihilation. He who has spread out that vast horizon, who raised those lofty mountains whose icy tops the sun is even now gilding, is also He who made my heart to beat, and my mind to think.

No! My friend is not annihilated. Whatever may be the barrier that separates us, I shall see him again. My hopes are based on no mere syllogism. The flight of an insect suffices to persuade me. And often the prospect of the surrounding country, the perfume of the air, and an indescribable charm which is spread around me, so raise my thoughts, that an invincible proof of immortality forces itself upon my soul, and fills it to the full.

XXII.

Jenny.

THE chapter I have just written had often presented itself to my pen, but I had as often rejected it. I had promised myself that I would only allow the cheerful phase of my soul to show itself in this book. But this project, like many others, I was forced to abandon. I hope the sensitive reader will pardon me for having asked his tears ; and if any one thinks I should have omitted this chapter, he can tear it from his copy, or even throw the whole book on the fire.

Enough for me, dear Jenny, that thy heart approves it, thou best and best-beloved of women, best and best-beloved of sisters. To thee I dedicate my work. If it please thee, it will please all gentle and delicate hearts. And if thou wilt pardon the follies into which, albeit against my will, I sometimes fall, I will brave all the critics of the universe.

XXIII.

The Picture Gallery.

ONE word only upon our next engraving.

It represents the family of the unfortunate Ugolino, dying of hunger. Around him are his sons. One of them lies motionless at his feet. The rest stretch their enfeebled arms towards him, asking for bread ; while the wretched father, leaning against a pillar of his prison, his eyes fixed and haggard, his countenance immovable, dies a double death, and suffers all that human nature can endure.

And there is the brave Chevalier d'Assas, dying, by an effort of courage and heroism unknown in our days, under a hundred bayonets.

And thou who weepest under the palm-trees, poor negro woman! thou, whom some barbarous fellow has betrayed and deserted, nay, worse, whom he has had the brutality to sell as a vile slave, notwithstanding thy love and devotion, notwithstanding the pledge of affection thou hast borne at thy breast, — I will not pass before thine image without rendering to thee the homage due to thy tenderness and thy sorrows.

Let us pause a moment before the other picture. It is a young shepherdess tending her flock alone on the heights of the Alps. She sits on an old willow trunk, bleached by many winters. Her feet are covered by the broad leaves of a tuft of *cacalia*, whose lilac blossoms bloom above her head. Lavender, wild thyme, the anemone, centaury, and flowers which are cultivated with care in our hot-houses and gardens, and which grow in all their native beauty on the Alps, form the gay carpet on which her sheep wander.

Lovely shepherdess! tell me where is the lovely spot thou callest thy home. From what far-off sheepfold didst thou set out at daybreak this morning? Could I not go thither and live with thee?

But alas, the sweet tranquillity thou enjoyest will soon vanish! The demon of war, not content with desolating cities, will ere long carry anxiety and alarm to thy solitary retreat. Even now I see the soldiers advancing: they climb height after height, as they march upward towards the clouds. The cannons' roar is heard high above the thunder-clap.

Fly, O shepherdess! Urge on thy flock! Hide thee in the farthest caves, for no longer is repose to be found on this sad earth!

XXIV.

Painting and Music.

I DO not know how it is, but of late my chapters have always ended in a mournful strain. In vain do I begin by fixing my eyes on some agreeable object ; in vain do I embark when all is calm : a sudden gale soon drifts me away. To put an end to an agitation which deprives me of the mastery of my ideas, and to quiet the beating of a heart too much disturbed by so many touching images, I see no remedy but a dissertation. Yes, thus will I steel my heart.

And the dissertation shall be about painting, for I cannot at this moment expatiate upon any other subject. I cannot altogether descend from the point I just now reached. Besides, painting is to me what Uncle Toby's hobby-horse was to him.[1]

I would say a few words, by the way, upon the question of preëminence between the charming arts of painting and music. I would cast my grain into the balance, were it but a grain of sand, a mere atom.

It is urged in favor of the painter, that he leaves his works behind him ; that his pictures outlive him, and immortalize his memory.

In reply to this we are reminded that musical composers also leave us their operas and oratorios.

But music is subject to fashion, and painting is not. The musical passages that deeply affected our forefathers seem

---

[1] The reader will probably have been reminded of the " Sentimental Journey " before reaching this proof of our author's acquaintance with the writings of Sterne.

H. A.

simply ridiculous to the amateurs of our own day; and they are placed in absurd farces to furnish laughter for the nephews of those whom they once made to weep.

Raphael's pictures will enchant our descendants as greatly as they did our forefathers.

This is my grain of sand.

XXV.

An Objection.

"BUT what," said Madame de Haut-castel to me one day, — "what if the music of Cherubini or Cimarosa differs from that of their predecessors? What care I if the music of the past make me laugh, so long as that of the present day touch me by its charms? Is it at all essential to my happiness that my pleasures should resemble those of my great-grandmother? Why talk to me of painting, an art which is only enjoyed by a very small class of persons, while music enchants every living creature?"

I hardly know at this moment how one could reply to this observation, which I did not foresee when I began my chapter.

Had I foreseen it, perhaps I should not have undertaken that dissertation. And pray do not imagine that you discover in this *objection* the artifice of a musician, for upon my honor I am none, Heaven be my witness, and all those who have heard me play the violin !

But, even supposing the merits of the two arts to be equal, we must not be too hasty in concluding that the merits of the *disciples* of Painting and Music are therefore balanced. We see children play the harpsichord as if they were *maestri*, but no one has ever been a good painter at twelve years old. Painting, besides taste and feeling, requires an amount of thoughtfulness that musicians can dispense with. Any day may you hear men who are well nigh destitute of head and heart, bring out from a violin or harp the most ravishing sounds.

The human ANIMAL may be taught to play the harpsichord, and when it has learned of a good master, the soul can travel at her ease while sounds with which she does not concern herself are mechanically produced by the fingers. But the simplest thing in the world cannot be painted without the aid of all the faculties of the soul.

If, however, any one should take it into his head to ply me with a distinction between the composition and the performance of music, I confess that he would give me some little difficulty. Ah, well! were all writers of essays quite candid they would all conclude as I am doing. When one enters upon the examination of a question, a dogmatic tone is generally assumed, because there has been a secret decision beforehand, just as I, notwithstanding my hypocritical impartiality, had decided in favor of painting. But discussion awakens objections, and everything ends with doubt.

XXVI.

Raphael.

NOW that I am more tranquil, I will endeavor to speak calmly of the two portraits that follow the picture of the shepherdess of the Alps.

Raphael! Who but thyself could paint thy portrait ; who but thyself would have dared attempt it? Thy open countenance, beaming with feeling and intellect, proclaims thy·character and thy genius.

To gratify thy shade, I have placed beside thee the portrait of thy mistress, whom the men of all generations will hold answerable for the loss of the sublime works of which art has been deprived by thy premature death.

When I examine the portrait of Raphael,

I feel myself penetrated by an almost religious respect for that great man, who, in the flower of his age, excelled the ancients, and whose pictures are at once the admiration and the despair of modern artists. My soul, in admiring it, is moved with indignation against that Italian who preferred her love to her lover, and who extinguished at her bosom that heavenly flame, that divine genius.

Unhappy one! Knewest thou not that Raphael had announced a picture superior even to that of the *Transfiguration?* Didst thou not know that thine arms encircled the favorite of nature, the father of enthusiasm, a sublime genius. . . . a divinity ?

While my soul makes these observations, her companion, whose eyes are attentively fixed upon the lovely face of that fatal beauty, feels quite ready to forgive her the death of Raphael.

In vain my soul upbraids this extravagant weakness ; she is not listened to at
all. On such occasions a strange dialogue
arises between the two, which terminates
too often in favor of the bad principles, and
of which I reserve a sample for another
chapter.

And if, by the way, my soul had not at
that moment abruptly closed the inspection of the gallery, if she had given the
OTHER time to contemplate the rounded
and graceful features of the beautiful Ro-
man lady, my intellect would have miser-
ably lost its supremacy.

And if, at that critical moment I had
suddenly obtained the favor bestowed upon
the fortunate Pygmalion, without having
the least spark of the genius which makes
me pardon Raphael his errors, it is just
possible that I should have succumbed as
he did.

XXVII.

A Perfect Picture.

MY engravings, and the paintings of which I have spoken, fade away into nothing at the first glance bestowed upon the next picture. The immortal works of Raphael and Correggio, and of the whole Italian school, are not to be compared to it. Hence it is that when I accord to an amateur the pleasure of travelling with me, I always keep this until the last as a special luxury, and ever since I first exhibited this sublime picture to connoisseurs and to ignorant, to men of the world, to artists, to women, to children, to animals even, I have always found the spectators, whoever they might be, show, each in his own way, signs of pleasure and surprise, so admirably is nature rendered therein.

And what picture could be presented to you, gentlemen ; what spectacle, ladies, could be placed before your eyes more certain of gaining your approval than the faithful portraiture of yourselves ? The picture of which I speak is a mirror, and no one has as yet ventured to criticise it. It is to all who look on it a perfect picture, in depreciation of which not a word can be said.

You will at once admit that it should be regarded as one of the wonders of the world.

I will pass over in silence the pleasure felt by the natural philosopher in meditating upon the strange phenomena presented by light as it reproduces upon that polished surface all the objects of nature. A mirror offers to the sedentary traveller a thousand interesting reflections, a thousand observations which render it at once a useful and precious article.

Ye whom Love has held or still holds under his sway, learn that it is before a mirror that he sharpens his darts, and contemplates his cruelties. There it is that he plans his manœuvres, studies his tactics, and prepares himself for the war he wishes to declare. There he practices his killing glances and little affectations, and sly poutings, just as a player practices, with himself for spectator, before appearing in public.

A mirror, being always impartial and true, brings before the eyes of the beholder the roses of youth and the wrinkles of age, without calumny and without flattery. It alone among the councilors of the great, invariably tells them the truth.

It was this recommendation that made me desire the invention of a moral mirror, in which all men might see themselves, with their virtues and their vices. I even thought of offering a prize to some academy for this discovery, when riper reflection proved to me that such an invention would be useless.

Alas! how rare it is for ugliness to recognize itself and break the mirror! In vain are looking-glasses multiplied around us which reflect light and truth with geometrical exactness. As soon as the rays reach our vision and paint us as we are, self-love slips its deceitful prism between us and our image, and presents a divinity to us.

And of all the prisms that have existed since the first that came from the hands of the immortal Newton, none has possessed so powerful a refractive force, or produced such pleasing and lively colors, as the prism of self-love.

Now, seeing that ordinary looking-glasses record the truth in vain, and that they cannot make men see their own imperfections, every one being satisfied with his face, what would a moral mirror avail?

Few people would look at it, and no one would recognize himself. None save philosophers would spend their time in examining themselves, — I even have my doubts about the philosophers.

Taking the mirror as we find it, I hope no one will blame me for ranking it above all the pictures of the Italian school.

Ladies, whose taste cannot be faulty, and whose opinion should decide the question, generally upon entering a room let their first glance fall upon this picture.

A thousand times have I seen ladies, aye, and gallants, too, forget at a ball their lovers and their mistresses, the dancing, and all the pleasures of the fete, to contemplate with evident complaisance this enchanting picture, and honoring it even, from time to time, in the midst of the liveliest quadrille, with a look.

Who then can dispute the rank that I accord to it among the masterpieces of the art of Apelles?

XXVIII.

The Upset Carriage.

I HAD at last nearly reached my bureau. So close was I, that had I stretched out my arm I could have touched the corner nearest to me. But at this very moment I was on the verge of seeing the fruit of all my labors destroyed, and of losing my life. I should pass over in silence the accident that happened to me, for fear of discouraging other travellers, were it not that it is so difficult to upset such a post-chaise as I employ, that it must be allowed that one must be uncommonly unlucky — as unlucky, indeed, as it is my lot to be — to be exposed to a like danger.

There I was, stretched at full length upon the ground, completely upset, and it was done so quickly, so unexpectedly, that I should have been almost tempted to question the cause of my abject position, had not a singing in my ears and a sharp pain in my left shoulder too plainly demonstrated it.

This was again the OTHER, who had played a trick upon me.

Startled by the voice of a poor man who suddenly asked alms at my door, and by the voice of Rose, my other half suddenly turned the arm-chair sharply round, before my soul had time to warn it that a piece of brick, which served as a drag, was gone. The jerk was so violent that my post-chaise was quite thrown from its centre of gravity, and turned over upon me.

This was, I must own, one of the occasions upon which I had most to complain of my soul. For instead of being vexed at herself for having been absent, and scolding her companion for its hurry, she

so far forgot herself as to give way to the
most animal resentment, and to insult the
poor fellow cruelly.

"Idle rascal," she said, "go and work."
(An execrable apostrophe this, the invention of miserly, heartless Mammon.)

"Sir," replied the man, hoping to soften
my heart, "I come from Chambéry."

"So much the worse for you."

"I am James. You saw me when you
were in the country. I used to drive the
sheep into the fields."

"And what do you do here?" My soul
began to regret the harshness of my first
words; I almost think she regretted them
a moment before they were uttered. In
like manner, when one meets in the road a
rut or puddle, one sees it, but has not time
to avoid it.

Rose finished the work of bringing me
to good sense and repentance. She had
recognized Jem, who had often shared his

crust with her, and she testified by her caresses, her remembrance and gratitude.

Meanwhile, Joannetti, who had gathered together what was left of my dinner, his own share, gave it at once to Jem.

Poor Joannetti !

Thus it is that in my journey I get lessons of philosophy and humanity from my servant and my dog.

XXIX.

Misfortune.

BEFORE proceeding farther, I wish to remove a suspicion which may have crossed the minds of my readers.

I would not for all the world be suspected of having undertaken this journey just because I did not know how to spend my time, and was in a manner compelled thereto by circumstances. I here affirm, and swear by all that is dear to me, that I projected it long before the event took place which deprived me of my liberty for forty-two days. This forced retirement only served as an opportunity for setting out sooner than I had intended.

This gratuitous protestation will, I know, appear suspicious in the eyes of some.

But those who are so ready to suspect are just the persons who will not read this book. They have enough to do at home and at their friends', plenty of other business to attend to. And good, honest folk will believe me.

Still, I freely admit that I should have preferred another season for my journey, and that I should have chosen for its execution Lent rather than the Carnival. The philosophical reflections, however, that have come to me from above have greatly aided me in supporting the loss of those pleasures which Turin offers at this noisy and exciting time.

It is certain, I have thought to myself, that the walls of my chamber are not so magnificently decorated as those of a ball-room. The silence of my cottage is far less agreeable than the pleasing sounds of music and dancing. But among the brilliant personages one meets in those festive scenes, there are certainly some who are more sick at heart than I am.

And why should I picture to myself those who are more happily circumstanced than it is my lot to be, while the world swarms with those who are worse off? Instead of transporting myself in fancy to that sumptuous dancing-hall, where so many beauties are eclipsed by the young Eugénie, I need only pause a moment in one of the streets, that lead thither, if I would learn how happy is my fate.

For, under the porticos of those magnificent apartments, lie a crowd of wretched people, half-naked, and ready to die from cold and misery. What a spectacle is here! Would that this page of my book were known throughout the universe! Would that every one knew that in this opulent city a host of wretched beings sleep, without covering, in the coldest winter nights, and with no pillow but the corner-stone of a street, or the steps of a palace.

Here, again, is a group of children, crouching together for protection from the deadly cold ; and here a trembling woman, who has no voice left to complain with: The passers-by come and go without being touched by a spectacle with which they are so familiar. The noise of carriages, the shouts of intemperance, the ravishing sounds of music, mingle not unfrequently with the wails of those unhappy creatures, and fill the ear with doleful discord.

XXX.

Charity.

WERE any one to pass a hasty judgment upon a city, taking my last
chapter as a criterion, he would err greatly.
I have spoken of the poor we meet with, of
their pitiful lamentations, and of the indifference with which many regard them.
But I have said nothing of the multitude
of charitable persons who sleep while others
seek amusement, and who rise at dawn,
unobserved and unostentatiously, to succor
the unfortunate.

This aspect of city life must not be
passed by in silence. I will write it on the
reverse of the page I was anxious everybody should read.

After having divided their good things

with their brethren, after having poured balm into hearts chafed by sorrow, you may see them enter the churches, while wearied vice sleeps upon eider-down, to offer up. their prayers to God, and to thank Him for his mercies. The light of a solitary lamp still struggles in the sanctuary with the daylight; but they are already prostrate before the altar. And the Almighty, angered by the hard-hearted selfishness of men, witholds his threatening hand.

XXXI.

Inventory.

I COULD not help saying a word in my journey about those poor creatures, for the thought of them has often come across me on my way, and turned the current of my reflections. Sometimes, struck with the difference between their case and my own, I have suddenly stopped my travelling-carriage, and thought my chamber extravagantly embellished! What superfluous luxury! Six chairs, two tables, a bureau, and a looking-glass! What vain display! My bed above all things, my rose and white bed, with its two mattresses, seemed to rival the magnificence and effeminacy of Asiatic monarchs.

These meditations made me indifferent

to the pleasures that had been forbidden me.   And, as I went on from one reflection to another, my fit of philosophy became so serious that I could have seen a ball going on in the next room, and heard the sound of violins and flutes without stirring.   I could have heard Marchesini's melodious voice, that voice which has so often transported me, yes, I could have listened to it without being moved.   Nay, more, I could have gazed upon the most beauteous woman in Turin, upon Eugénie herself, adorned from head to foot by the hands of Mademoiselle Rapoux,[1] without emotion. But, of this last, I must confess myself not quite sure.

[1] A fashionable milliner of the time.

XXXII.

Misanthropy.

BUT, gentlemen, allow me to ask a question. Do you enjoy balls and plays as much as you used to do? As for me, I avow that for some time past crowded assemblies have inspired me with a kind of terror. When in their midst, I am assailed by an ominous dream. In vain I try to shake it off; like the dream of *Athalie*, it constantly returns. Perhaps this is because the soul, overwhelmed at the present moment by dark fancies and painful pictures, sees nothing but sadness around it, just as a disordered stomach turns the most wholesome food into poison. However this may be, my dream is as follows. When I am at one of these fêtes, among a crowd of kind, good-natured men, who dance and sing, who weep at trage- dies, and are full of frankness and cordial- ity, I say to myself : —

"If suddenly a white bear, a philoso- pher, a tiger, or some other animal of this kind were to enter, and ascending to the orchestra, were to shout out furiously : 'Wretched beings! Listen to the truth that comes from my lips! You are op- pressed! You are the slaves of tyrants ! You are wretched and heart-sick! Awake from your lethargy !

"'Musicians, break your instruments about your heads, and let each one of you arm himself with a poniard. Think no more about holidays and rejoicings. Climb into the boxes, and stab their oc- cupants, one and all. And let the women steep their timid hands in blood.

"'Quit this room, for you are free! Tear your king from his throne, and your God from his sanctuary.'

"Well, and how many of these charming men will obey this tiger's voice. How many of them thought, perhaps, of such deeds before they entered? Who can tell? Was there no dancing in Paris five years ago?"

Joannetti! shut the door and windows! I do not wish to see the light! Let no one enter my room. Put my sword within reach. Go out yourself, and keep away from me.

7

XXXIII.

Consolation.

NO, no! Stay, Joannetti, my good
fellow! And you too, Rose, you
who guess what are my sorrows, and
soften them by your caresses, come!

V forms the resting-place.

XXXIV.

Correspondence.

THE upset of my post-chaise has rendered the reader the service of shortening my journey by a good dozen chapters, for, upon getting up, I found myself close to my bureau, and saw that I had no time left for any observations upon a number of engravings and pictures which had yet to be surveyed, and which might have lengthened my excursions into the realm of painting.

Leaving to the right the portraits of Raphael and his mistress, the Chevalier d'Assas and the Shepherdess of the Alps, and taking the left, the side on which the window is situated, my bureau comes into view. It is the first and the most prominent object the traveller's eyes light upon, taking the route I have indicated.

It is surmounted by a few shelves that serve as a book-case, and the whole is terminated by a bust which completes the pyramid, and contributes more than any other object to the adornment of this region.

Upon opening the first drawer to the left, we find an inkstand, paper of all kinds, pens ready mended, and sealing-wax; all which set the most indolent person longing to write.

I am sure, dear Jenny, that if you chanced to open this drawer, you would reply to the letter I wrote you a year ago.

In the opposite drawer lies a confused heap of materials for a touching history of the prisoner of Pignerol,[1] which, my dear friends, you will ere long read.

Between these two drawers is a recess

[1] This work was not published.

into which I throw whatever letters I receive. All that have reached me during the last ten years are there. The oldest of them are arranged according to date in several packets ; the new ones lie pell-mell. Besides these, I have several dating from my early boyhood.

How great a pleasure it is to behold again through the medium of these letters the interesting scenes of our early years, to be once again transported into those happy days that we shall see no more !

How full is my heart, and how deeply tinged with sadness is its joy, as my eyes wander over those words traced by one who is gone forever ! That handwriting is his, and it was his heart that guided his hand. It was to me that he addressed this letter, and this letter is all that is left of him !

When I put my hand into this recess, I seldom leave the spot for the whole day.

In like manner, a traveller will pass rapidly through whole provinces of Italy, making a few hurried and trivial observations on the way, and upon reaching Rome will take up his abode there for months.

This is the richest vein in the mine I am exploring. How changed I find my ideas and sentiments, and how altered do my friends appear when I examine them as they were in days gone by, and as they are now! In these mirrors of the past I see them in mortal agitation about plans which no longer disturb them.

Here I find an event announced which we evidently looked upon as a great misfortune; but the end of the letter is wanting, and the circumstance is so entirely forgotten that I cannot now make out what the matter was which so concerned us. We were possessed by a thousand prejudices. We knew nothing of the world, and of men. But then, how warm was our intercourse!

How intimate our friendship! How unbounded our confidence!

In our ignorance there was bliss. But now, — ah! all is now changed. We have been compelled, as others, to read the human heart; and truth, falling like a bomb into the midst of us, has forever destroyed the enchanted palace of illusion.

XXXV.

The Withered Rose.

IF the subject were worth the trouble, I could readily write a chapter upon that dry rose. It is a flower of last year's carnival. I gathered it myself in the Valentino.[1] And in the evening, an hour before the ball was to begin, I bore it, full of hope, and agreeably excited, to Madame Hautcastel, for her acceptance. She took it, and without looking at it or me, placed it upon her toilette-table. And how could she have given *me* any of her attention? She was engaged in looking at herself.

[1] The botanical garden of Turin.

There she stood before a large mirror ; her hair was ornamented for a fête, and the decorations of her dress were undergoing their final arrangement. She was so fully occupied, her attention was so totally absorbed by the ribbons, gauzes, and all sorts of finery that lay in heaps before her, that I did not get a look or any sign of recognition. There was nothing for me but resignation. I held out humbly in my hand a number of pins arranged in order. But her pincushion being more within reach, she took them from her pincushion, and when I brought my hand nearer, she took them from my hand, quite indifferently, and in taking them up she would feel about for them with the tips of her fingers, without taking her eyes from the glass, lest she should lose sight of herself.

For some time I held behind her a second mirror that she might judge the better how her dress became her, and as her face reflected itself from one glass to another, I saw a prospective of coquettes, no one of whom paid me the least attention. In a word, I must confess that my rose and I cut a very poor figure.

At last I lost all patience, and unable longer to control the vexation that preyed upon me, I put down the looking-glass I had been holding, and went out angrily without taking leave.

"O! you are going?" she said, turning so as to see her figure in profile. I made no answer, but I listened some time at the door to see what effect my abrupt departure would have.

"Do you not see," she said to her maid, after a moment's silence, "that this caraco, particularly the lower part, is much too large at the waist, and will want pinning?"

Why and wherefore that rose is upon my shelf, I shall certainly not explain, for, as I said before, a withered rose does not deserve a chapter.

And pray observe, ladies, that I make no reflection upon the adventure with the rose. I do not say whether Madame de Hautcastel did well or otherwise in preferring her dress to me, or whether I had any right to a better reception.

I take special care to deduce therefrom no general conclusions about the reality, the strength, and the duration of the affection of ladies for their friends. I am content to cast this chapter (since it is one) into the world with the rest of my journey, without addressing it to any one, and without recommending it to any one.

·I will only add, gentlemen, a word of counsel. Impress well upon your minds this fact, that your mistress is no longer yours on the day of a ball.

As soon as dressing begins, a lover is no more thought of than a husband would be; and the ball takes the place of a lover.

Every one knows how little a husband

gains by enforcing his love. Take your trouble, then, patiently, cheerfully.

And, my dear sir, do not deceive yourself; if a lady welcome you at a ball, it is not as a lover that you are received, for you are a husband — but as a part of the ball; and you are therefore but a fraction of her new conquest. You are the decimal of a lover. Or, it may be, you dance well, and so give éclat to her graces. After all, perhaps, the most flattering way in which you can regard her kind welcome is to consider that she hopes by treating as her cavalier a man of parts like yourself, to excite the jealousy of her companions. Were it not for that she would not notice you at all.

It amounts then to this. You must resign yourself to your fate, and wait until the husband's *rôle* is played. I know those who would be glad to get off at so cheap a rate.

XXXVI.

The Library.

I PROMISED to give a dialogue between my soul and the OTHER. But
there are some chapters which elude me,
as it were, or rather, there are others which
flow from my pen *nolens volens,* and de-
range my plans. Among these is one
about my library; and I will make it as
short as I can. Our forty-two days will
soon be ended; and even were it not so,
a similar period would not suffice to com-
plete the description of the rich country
in which I travel so pleasantly.

My library, then, is composed of novels,
if I must make the confession; of novels
and a few choice poets.

As if I had not troubles enough of my

own, I share those of a thousand imaginary personages, and I feel them as acutely as my own. How many tears have I shed for that poor Clarissa,[1] and for Charlotte's [2] lover !

But if I go out of my way in search of unreal afflictions, I find in return, such virtue, kindness, and disinterestedness in this imaginary world as I have never yet found united in the real world around me. I meet with a woman after my heart's desire, free from whim, lightness, and affectation. I say nothing about beauty ; this I can leave to my imagination, and picture her faultlessly beautiful. And then, closing the book, which no longer keeps pace with my ideas, I take the fair one by the hand, and we travel together over a country a thousand times more delightful than Eden itself. What painter could represent the

[1] Richardson's *Clarissa Harlowe.*
[2] Goethe's *Werther.*

fairy land in which I have placed the goddess of my heart? What poet could ever
describe the lively and manifold sensations
I experience in those enchanted regions?

How often have I cursed that Cleveland,[1]
who is always embarking upon new troubles
which he might very well avoid! I cannot endure that book with its long list of
calamities. But if I open it by way of distraction, I cannot help devouring it to the
end.

For how could I leave that poor man
among the Abaquis? What would become
of him in the hands of those savages?
Still less dare I leave him in his attempt
to escape from captivity.

Indeed, I so enter into his sorrows, I am
so interested in him and in his unfortunate
family, that the sudden appearance of the
ferocious Ruintons makes my hair stand
on end. When I read that passage a cold

[1] *Cleveland*, by the Abbé Prévost.

perspiration covers me, and my fright is as lively and real as if I was going to be roasted and eaten by the monsters myself.

When I have had enough of tears and love, I turn to some poet, and set out again for a new world.

XXXVII.

Another World.

FROM the Argonautic expedition to the Assembly of Notables; from the bottom of the nethermost pit to the furthest fixed star beyond the Milky Way; to the confines of the Universe; to the gates of chaos; thus far extends the vast field over the length and breadth of which I leisurely roam. I lack nor time nor space. Thither, conducted by Homer, by Milton, by Virgil, by Ossian, I transport my existence.

All the events that have taken place between these two epochs; all the countries, all the worlds, all the beings that have existed between these two boundaries, — all are mine, all as lawfully belong to me as the

8

ships that entered the Piræus belonged to a certain Athenian.

Above all the rest do I love the poets who carry me back to the remotest antiquity. The death of the ambitious Agamemnon, the madness of Orestes, and the tragical history of the heaven-persecuted family of the Atrides, inspire me with a terror that all the events of modern times could not excite in my breast.

Behold the fatal urn which contains the ashes of Orestes! Who would not shudder at the sight? Electra, unhappy sister! be comforted, for it is Orestes himself who bears the urn, and the ashes are those of his enemies.

No longer are their banks like those of Xanthus or the Scamander. No longer do we visit plains such as those of Hesperia or Arcadia. Where are now the isles of Lemnos and Crete? Where the famous labyrinth? Where is the rock that forlorn

Ariadne washed with her tears? Theseus is seen no more; Hercules is gone forever. The men, aye, and the heroes of our day are but pigmies.

When I would visit a scene full of enthusiasm, and put forth all the strength of my imagination, I cling boldly to the flowing robe of the sublime blind poet of Albion at the moment when he soars heavenward, and dares approach the throne of the Eternal. What muse was able to sustain him in a flight so lofty that no man before him ever ventured to raise his eyes so high? From heaven's dazzling pavement which avaricious Mammon looked down upon with envious eyes, I pass, horror-stricken, to the vast caverns of Satan's sojourn. I take my place at the infernal council, mingle with the host of rebellious spirits, and listen to their discourse.

But here I must confess a weakness for which I have often reproached myself.

I cannot help taking a certain interest in Satan, thus hurled headlong from heaven. (I am speaking, of course, of *Milton's* Satan.) While I blame the obstinacy of the rebel angel, the firmness he shows in the midst of his exceeding great misery, and the grandness of his courage, inspire me, against my will, with admiration. Although not ignorant of the woe resulting from the direful enterprise that led him to force the gate of hell and to trouble the home of our first parents, I cannot for a moment, do what I will, wish he may perish in the confusion of chaos on his way. I even think I could willingly help him, did not shame withhold me. I follow his every movement, and take as much pleasure in travelling with him as if I were in very good company. In vain I consider that after all he is a devil on his way to the ruin of the human race, that he is a thorough democrat, not after the manner of those of

Athens, but of Paris. All this does not cure me of my prejudice in his favor.

How vast was his project! How great the boldness displayed in its execution!

When the thrice-threefold gates of hell fly open before him, and the dark, boundless ocean discloses itself in all its horror at his feet, with undaunted eye he surveys the realm of chaos, and then, opening his sail-broad wings, precipitates himself into the abyss.[1]

To me this passage is one of the noblest efforts of imagination, and one of the most splendid journeys ever made, next to *the journey round my room.*

[1] Some freedom of translation is, perhaps, pardonable here. Our author, depending, it would seem, upon his memory, gives Satan wings large enough "to cover a whole army" It was "the extended wings" of the gates of hell, not of Satan, that Milton describes as wide enough to admit a "bannered host." *Paradise Lost,* ii. 885. H. A.

XXXVIII.

The Bust.

I SHOULD never end if I tried to describe a thousandth part of the strange events I meet with when I travel in my library. The voyages of Cook and the observations of his fellow-travellers Banks and Solander are nothing compared with my adventures in this one district. Indeed, I think I could spend my life there in a kind of rapture, were it not for the bust I have already mentioned, upon which my eyes and thoughts always fix themselves at last, whatever may be the position of my soul. And when my soul is violently agitated, or a prey to despair, a glance at this bust suffices to restore the troubled being to its natural state. It sounds the chord upon which I keep in tune the harmonies, and correct the discords of the sensations and perceptions of which my being is made up. How striking the likeness! Those are the features nature gave to the best of men. O, that the sculptor had been able to bring to view his noble soul, his genius, his character! But what am I attempting! Is it here that his praise should be recorded? Do I address myself to the men that surround me? Ah! what concern is it of theirs?

I am contented to bend before thy image, O best of fathers! Alas, that this should be all that is left me of thee and of my father-land! Thou quittedst the earth when crime was about to invade it; and so heavy are the ills that oppress thy family, that we are constrained to regard thy loss as a blessing. Many would have been the evils a longer life would have brought upon thee! And dost thou, O my father, dost thou, in thine abode of bliss, know the lot of thy family! Knowest thou that thy children are exiled from the country thou hast served with so much zeal and integrity for sixty years?

Dost thou know that they are forbidden to visit thy grave? But tyranny has not been able to deprive them of the most precious part of thy heritage, the record of thy virtues, and the force of thine example. In the midst of the torrent of crime which has borne their father-land and their patrimony to ruin, they have steadfastly remained united in the path marked out for them by thee. And when it shall be given them to prostrate themselves once more beside thy tomb, thou shalt see in them thine obedient children.

XXXIX.

A Dialogue.

I PROMISED a dialogue, and I will keep my word.

It was daybreak. The rays of the sun were gilding the summit of Mount Viso, and the tops of the highest hills on the island beneath our feet. My soul was already awake. This early awakening may have been the effect of those night visions which often excite in her a fatiguing and useless agitation : or perhaps the carnival, then drawing to a close, was the secret cause ; for this season of pleasure and folly influences the human organization much as do the phases of the moon and the conjunction of certain planets. However this may be, my soul was awake, and wide awake, when she shook off the bands of sleep.

For some time she had shared, though confusedly, the sensations of the OTHER: but she was still encumbered by the swathes of night and sleep; and these swathes seemed to her transformed into gauze and fine linen and Indian lawn. My poor soul was, as it were, enwrapped in all this paraphernalia, and the god of sleep, that he might hold her still more firmly under his sway, added to these bonds disheveled tresses of flaxen hair, ribbon bows, and pearl necklaces. Really it was pitiful to see her struggle in these toils.

The agitation of the nobler part of myself communicated itself to the OTHER; and the latter, in its turn, reacted powerfully upon my soul.

I worked myself, at last, into a state which it would be hard to describe, while my soul, either sagaciously or by chance, hit upon a way of escaping from the gauzes by which it was being suffocated. I know

not whether she discovered an outlet, or
whether, which is a more natural conclusion, it occurred to her to raise them : at all
events, she found a means of egress from
the labyrinth. The tresses of disheveled
hair were still there ; but they were now
rather help than hindrance ; my soul seized
them, as a drowning man clutches the
sedge on a river's bank, but the pearl neck-
lace broke in the act, and the unstrung
pearls rolled on the sofa, and from the sofa
to Madame Hautcastel's floor (for my soul,
by an eccentricity for which it would be
difficult to give a reason, fancied she was
at that lady's house) ; then a great bunch
of violets fell to the ground, and my soul,
which then awoke, returned home, bringing with her common sense and reality.
She strongly disapproved, as you will readily imagine, of all that had passed in her
absence ; and here it is that the dialogue
begins which forms the subject of this
chapter.

Never had my soul been so ungraciously received. The complaints she thought fit to make at this critical moment fully sufficed to stir up domestic strife ; a revolt, a formal insurrection followed.

"What!" said my soul, "is it thus that during my absence, instead of restoring your strength by quiet sleep that you may be better able to do my bidding, you have the insolence (the expressing was rather strong) to give yourself up to transports which my authority has not sanctioned!"

Little accustomed to this haughty tone, the OTHER angrily answered : —

"Really, madame" (this madame was meant to remove from the discussion anything like familiarity), "really, this affectation of virtuous decorum is highly becoming to you! Is it not to the sallies of your imagination, and to your extravagant ideas, that I owe what in me displeases you? What right have you to go on those pleasant excursions so often, without taking me with you? Have I ever complained about your attending the meetings in the Empyrean or in the Elysian fields, your conversations with the celestial intelligences, your profound speculations (a little raillery here, you see), your castles in the air, and your transcendental systems? And have I not a right, when you leave me in this way, to enjoy the blessings bestowed upon me by Nature, and the pleasures she places before me?"

My soul, surprised at so much vivacity and eloquence, did not know how to reply. In order to settle the dispute amicably, she endeavored to veil with the semblance of good-nature the reproaches that had escaped her. But, that she might not seem to take the first steps towards reconciliation, she affected a formal tone. "*Madame,*" she said, with assumed cordiality. . . . . If the reader thought the word misplaced when addressed to my soul, what will he say of it now, if he call to mind the cause of the quarrel? But my soul did not feel the extreme absurdity of this mode of expression, so much does passion obscure the intellect! "Madame," she said, "nothing, be assured, would give me so much pleasure as to see you enjoy those pleasures of which your nature is susceptible, if even I did not participate in them, were it not that such pleasures are harmful to you, injuriously affecting the harmony which . . ." Here my soul was rudely interrupted, "No, no, I am not the dupe of your pretended kindness. The sojourn we are compelled to make together in this room in which we travel; the wound which I received, which still bleeds, and which nearly destroyed me, — is not all this the fruit of your overweening conceit and your barbarous prejudices? My comfort, my very existence, is counted as nothing when your passions sway you : and then, forsooth, you pretend that you take an interest in my welfare, and that your insults spring from friendship."

My soul saw very well that the part she was playing on this occasion was no flattering one. She began, too, to perceive that the warmth of the dispute had put the cause of it out of sight. Profiting from this circumstance, she caused a further distraction by saying to Joannetti, who at that moment entered the room, " Make some coffee ! " The noise of the cups attracted all the rebel's attention, who forthwith forgot everything else. In like manner we show children a toy to make them forget the unwholesome fruit for which they beg and stamp.

While the water was being heated, I insensibly fell asleep. I enjoyed that delightful sensation about which I have already entertained my readers, and which you experience when you feel yourself to be dozing. The agreeable rattling Joannetti made with the coffee-pot reëchoed in my brain, and set all my sensitive nerves vibrating, just as a single harp-string when struck will make the octaves resound.

At last I saw as it were, a shadow pass before me. I opened my eyes, and there stood Joannetti. Ah, what an aroma! How agreeable a surprise! Coffee! Cream! A pyramid of dry toast! Good reader, come, breakfast with me!

XL.

Imagination.

WHAT a wealth of delights has kind Nature given to those who can enjoy them. Who can count the innumerable phases they assume in different individuals, and at different periods of life! The confused remembrance of the pleasures of my boyhood sends a thrill through my heart. Shall I attempt to paint the joys of the youth whose soul glows with all the warmth of love, at an age when interest, ambition, hatred, and all the base passions that degrade and torment humanity are unknown to him, even by name?

During this age, too short, alas! the sun shines with a brightness it never displays in after-life; the air is then purer, the streams clearer and fresher, and nature has aspects, and the woods have paths, which in our riper age we never find again. O, what perfumes those flowers breathe ! How delicious are those fruits ! With what colors is the morning sky adorned ! Men are all good, generous, kind-hearted ; and women all lovely and faithful. On all sides we meet with cordiality, frankness, and unselfishness. Nature presents to us nothing but flowers, virtues, and pleasures.

The excitement of love, and the anticipation of happiness, do they not fill our hearts to the brim with emotions no less lively and various ?

The sight of nature and its contemplation, whether we regard it as a whole, or examine its details, opens to our reason an immense field of enjoyments. Soon the imagination, brooding over this sea of pleasures, increases their number and intensity. The various sensations so unite

and blend as to form new ones. Dreams
of glory mingle with the palpitations of
love. Benevolence moves hand in hand
with self-esteem. Melancholy, from time
to time, throws over us her solemn livery,
and changes our tears to joy. Thus the
perceptions of the mind, the feelings of the
heart, the very remembrance of sensations,
are inexhaustible sources of pleasure and
comfort to man. No wonder, then, that
the noise Joannetti made with the coffee-
pot, and the unexpected appearance of a
cup of cream, should have impressed me
so vividly and so agreeably.

XLI.

The Travelling-coat.

I PUT on my travelling-coat, after having examined it with a complacent eye; and forthwith resolved to write a chapter *ad hoc*, that I might make it known to the reader.

The form and usefulness of these garments being pretty generally known, I will treat specially of their influence upon the minds of travellers.

My winter travelling-coat is made of the warmest and softest stuff I could meet with. It envelops me entirely from head to foot, and when I am in my arm-chair, with my hands in my pockets, I am very like the statue of Vishnu one sees in the pagodas of India.

You may, if you will, tax me with prejudice when I assert the influence a traveller's costume exercises upon its wearer. At any rate I can confidently affirm with regard to this matter, that it would appear to me as ridiculous to take a single step of my journey round my room in uniform, with my sword at my side, as it would to go forth into the world in my dressing-gown. Were I to find myself in full military dress, not only should I be unable to proceed with my journey, but I really believe I should not be able to read what I have written about my travels, still less to understand it.

Does this surprise you? Do we not every day meet with people who fancy they are ill because they are unshaven, or because some one has thought they have looked poorly, and told them so? Dress has such influence upon men's minds that there are valetudinarians who think themselves in better health than usual when they have on a new coat and well-powdered wig. They deceive the public and themselves by their nicety about dress, until one finds some fine morning they have died in full fig, and their death startles everybody.

And in the class of men among whom I live, how many there are who, finding themselves clothed in uniform, firmly believe they are officers, until the unexpected appearance of the enemy shows them their mistake. And more than this, if it be the king's good pleasure to allow one of them to add to his coat a certain trimming, he straightway believes himself to be a general, and the whole army gives him the title without any notion of making fun of him! So great an influence has a coat upon the human imagination!

The following illustration will show still further the truth of my assertion.

It sometimes happened that they forgot to inform the Count de —— some days beforehand of the approach of his turn to mount guard. Early one morning, on the very day on which this duty fell to the Count, a corporal awoke him, and announced the disagreeable news. But the idea of getting up there and then, putting on his gaiters, and turning out without having thought about it the evening before, so disturbed him that he preferred reporting himself sick and staying at home all day. So he put on his dressing-gown, and sent away his barber. This made him look pale and ill, and frightened his wife and family. He really *did* feel a little poorly.

He told every one he was not very well, partly for the sake of appearances, and partly because he positively believed himself to be indisposed. Gradually the influence of the dressing-gown began to work.

The slops he was obliged to take upset his stomach. His relations and friends sent to ask after him. He was soon quite ill enough to take to his bed.

In the evening Dr. Ranson[1] found his pulse hard and feverish, and ordered him to be bled next day,

If the campaign had lasted a month longer, the sick man's case would have been past cure.

Now, who can doubt about the influence of travelling-coats upon travellers, if he reflect that poor Count de —— thought more than once that he was about to perform a journey to the other world for having inopportunely donned his dressing-gown in this?

[1] A popular Turin physician when the *Voyage* was written.

XLII.

Aspasia's Buskin.

I WAS sitting near my fire after dinner, enveloped in my " habit de voyage," and freely abandoning myself to · its influence: the hour for starting was, I knew, drawing nigh ; but the fumes generated by digestion rose to my brain, and so obstructed the channels along which thoughts glide on their way from the senses, that all communication between them was intercepted. And as my senses no longer transmitted any idea to my brain, the latter, in its turn, could no longer emit any of that electric fluid with which the ingenious Doctor Valli resuscitates dead frogs.

After reading this preamble, you will easily understand why my head fell on my chest, and why the muscles of the thumb and forefinger of my right hand, being no longer excited by the electric fluid, became so relaxed that a volume of the works of the Marquis Caraccioli, which I was holding tightly between these two fingers, imperceptibly eluded my grasp, and fell upon the hearth.

I had just had some callers, and my conversation with the persons who had left the room had turned upon the death of Dr. Cigna, an eminent physician then lately deceased. He was a learned and hard-working man, a good naturalist, and a famous botanist. My thoughts were occupied with the merits of this skillful man. "And yet," I said to myself, "were it possible for me to evoke the spirits of those whom he has, perhaps, dismissed to the other world, who knows but that his reputation might suffer some diminution?"

I travelled insensibly to a dissertation on medicine and the progress it has made since the time of Hippocrates. I asked myself whether the famous personages of antiquity who died in their beds, as Pericles, Plato, the celebrated Aspasia, and Hippocrates, died, after the manner of ordinary mortals, of some putrid or inflammatory fever; and whether they were bled, and crammed with specifics.

To say why these four personages came into my mind rather than any others, is out of my power; for who can give reasons for what he dreams? All that I can say is that my soul summoned the doctor of Cos, the doctor of Turin, and the famous statesman who did such great things, and committed such grave faults.

But as to his graceful friend, I humbly own that it was the OTHER who beckoned her to come. Still, however, when I think of the interview, I am tempted to feel some little pride, for it is evident that in this dream the balance in favor of reason was as four to one. Pretty fair this, methinks, for a lieutenant.

However this may be, whilst giving myself up to the reflections I have described, my eyes closed, and I fell fast asleep. But upon shutting my eyes, the image of the personages of whom I had been thinking, remained painted upon that delicate canvas we call memory; and these images, mingling in my brain with the idea of the evocation of the dead, it was not long before I saw advancing in procession Hippocrates, Plato, Pericles, Aspasia, and Doctor Cigna in his bob-wig.

I saw them all seat themselves in chairs ranged around the fire. Pericles alone remained standing to read the newspapers.

"If the discoveries of which you speak were true," said Hippocrates to the doctor, "and had they been as useful to the healing art as you affirm, I should have seen the number of those who daily descend to the gloomy realm of Pluto decrease; but the ratio of its inhabitants, according to the registers of Minos which I have myself verified, remains still the same as formerly."

Doctor Cigna turned to me and said: "You have without doubt heard these discoveries spoken of. You know that Harvey discovered the circulation of the blood; that the immortal Spallanzani explained the process of digestion, the mechanism of which is now well understood;" and he entered upon a long detail of all the discoveries connected with physic, and of the host of remedies for which we are indebted to chemistry: in short, he delivered an academical discourse in favor of modern medicine.

"But am I to believe," I replied, "that these great men were ignorant of all you have been telling them, and that their souls, having shuffled off this mortal coil, still meet with any obscurities in nature ?"

"Ah! how great is your error!" exclaimed the *proto-physician*[1] of the Peloponnesus. The mysteries of nature are as closely hidden from the dead as from the living. Of one thing we who linger on the banks of the Styx are certain, that He who created all things alone knows the great secret which men vainly strive to solve. And," added he, turning to the doctor, " do be persuaded by me to divest yourself of what still clings to you of the party-spirit you have brought with you from the sojourn of mortals. And since, seeing that Charon daily ferries over in his boat as many shades as heretofore, the labors of a thousand generations and all the discov-

---

[1] A title known at the Sardinian court.

eries men have made have not been able to
prolong their existence, let us not uselessly
weary ourselves in defending an art which,
among the dead, cannot even profit its
practitioners."

Thus, to my great amazement, spoke the
famous Hippocrates.

Doctor Cigna smiled ; and as spirits
can neither withstand evidence, nor silence truth, he not only agreed with Hippocrates, but, blushing after the manner of
disembodied intelligences, he protested
that he had himself always had his doubts.

Pericles, who had drawn near the window, heaved a deep sigh, the cause of which
I divined.   He was reading a number of
the " Moniteur," which announced the de-
cadence of the arts and sciences.   He
saw illustrious scholars desert their sublime conceptions to invent new crimes,
and shuddered at hearing a rabble herd
compare themselves with the heroes of

generous Greece; and this, forsooth, because they put to death, without shame or
remorse, venerable old men, women, and
children, and coolly perpetrated the black-
est and most useless crimes.

Plato, who had listened to our conversation without joining in it, and seeing it
brought to a sudden and unexpected close,
thus spoke: "I can readily understand
that the discoveries great men have made
in the various branches of natural science
do not forward the art of medicine, which
can never change the course of nature,
except at the cost of life. But this will
certainly not be so with the researches
that have been made in the study of
politics. Locke's inquiries into the nature
of the human understanding, the invention
of printing, the accumulated observations
drawn from history, the number of excellent books which have spread sound infor-
mation even among the lower orders, — so

many wonders must have contributed to make men better, and the happy republic I conceived, which the age in which I lived caused me to regard as an impracticable dream, no doubt now exists upon the earth?" At this question the honest doctor cast down his eyes, and only answered by tears. In wiping them with his pocket-handkerchief, he involuntarily moved his wig on one side, so that a part of his face was hidden by it. "Ye gods!" exclaimed Aspasia, with a scream, "how strange a sight! And is it a discovery of one of your great men that has led you to the idea of turning another man's skull into a head-dress?"

Aspasia, from whom our philosophical dissertations had elicited nothing but gapes, had taken up a magazine of fashions which lay on the chimney-piece, the leaves of which she had been turning over for some time when the doctor's wig made

10

her utter this exclamation. Finding the narrow, ricketty seat upon which she was sitting uncomfortable, she had, without the least ceremony, placed her two bare legs, which were adorned with bandelets, on the straw-bottomed chair between her and me, and rested her elbow upon the broad shoulders of Plato.

"It is no skull," said the doctor, addressing her, and taking off his wig, which he threw on the fire, "it is a wig, madam; and I know not why I did not cast this ridiculous ornament into the flames of Tartarus when first I came among you. But absurdities and prejudices adhere so closely to our miserable nature that they even follow us sometimes beyond the grave." I took singular pleasure in seeing the doctor thus abjure his physic and his wig at the same moment.

"I assure you," said Aspasia, "that most of the head-dresses represented in the

pages I have been turning over deserve
the same fate as yours, so very extravagant
are they."

The fair Athenian amused herself vastly
in looking over the engravings, and was
very reasonably surprised by the variety
and oddity of modern contrivances. One
figure, especially struck her. It was that
of a young lady with a really elegant head-
dress which Aspasia only thought somewhat too high. But the piece of gauze
that covered the neck was so very full you
could scarcely see half her face. Aspasia,
not knowing that these extraordinary
developments were produced by starch,
could not help showing a surprise which
would have been redoubled (but inversely),
had the gauze been transparent.

"But do explain," she said, "why
women of the present day seem to wear
dresses to hide rather than to clothe them.
They scarcely allow their faces to be seen,

those faces by which alone their sex is
to be guessed, so strangely are their bodies disfigured by the eccentric folds of
their garments. Among all the figures
represented in these pages, I do not find
one with the neck, arms, and legs bare.
How is it your young warriors are not
tempted to put an end to such a fashion?
It would appear," she added, "that the
virtue of the women of this age, which
they parade in all their articles of dress,
greatly surpasses that of my contempora-
ries."

As she ended these words, Aspasia
turned her eyes on me as if to ask a reply.
I pretended not to notice this, and in order
to give myself an absent air, took up the
tongs and pushed away among the embers
the shreds of the doctor's wig which had
escaped the flames. Observing presently
afterwards that one of the bandelets which
clasped Aspasia's buskin had come undone,

" Permit me," said I, " charming lady," —
and eagerly stooping, stretched out my
hands towards the chair on which I had
fancied I saw those legs about which even
great philosophers went into ecstacies.

I am persuaded that at this moment I
was very near genuine somnambulism, so
real was the movement of which I speak.
But Rose, who happened to be sleeping in
the chair, thought the movement was
meant for her, and jumping nimbly into
my arms, she drove back into Hades the
famous shades my travelling-coat had
summoned.

Liberty.

DELIGHTFUL realm of Imagination, which the benevolent Being has bestowed upon man to console him for the disappointments he meets with in real life.

This day, certain persons on whom I am dependent affect to restore me to liberty. As if they had ever deprived me of it! As if it were in their power to snatch it from me for a single moment, and to hinder me from traversing, at my own good pleasure, the vast space that ever lies open before me! They have forbidden me to go at large in a city, a mere speck, and have left open to me the whole universe, in which immensity and eternity obey me.

I am now free, then; or rather, I must enter again into bondage. The yoke of

office is again to weigh me down, and
every step I take must conform with the
exigencies of politeness and duty. Fortunate shall I be if some capricious goddess
do not again make me forget both, and if I
escape from this new and dangerous captivity.

O why did they not allow me to finish
my captivity! Was it as a punishment
that I was exiled to my chamber, to that
delightful country in which abound all the
riches and enjoyments of the world? As
well might they consign a mouse to a
granary.

Still, never did I more clearly perceive
that I am double than I do now. Whilst
I regret my imaginary joys, I feel myself
consoled. I am borne along by an unseen
power which tells me I need the pure air,
and the light of heaven, and that solitude is
like death. Once more I don my custom-
ary garb; my door opens; I wander under

the spacious porticos of the Strada della Po; a thousand agreeable visions float before my eyes. Yes, there is that mansion, that door, that staircase! I thrill with expectation.

In like manner the act of slicing a lemon gives you a foretaste that makes your mouth water.

Poor ANIMAL! Take care!

The Sins Of The Family

THE SINS OF THE FAMILY:

𝔅eing 𝔖ermons

Preached in the Parish Church of S. Michael, Alnwick,

On Sunday Evenings during Lent, 1871.

BY

REV. E. B. TROTTER, M.A.,

THOMAS LAURIE:

LONDON, 30, NEW BRIDGE STREET, E.C.

EDINBURGH, 38, COCKBURN STREET.

EDINBURGH :
COMMERCIAL PRINTING COMPANY,
22 HOWE STREET.

PREFACE.

THESE Sermons are published by request. There was no intention of their going beyond the Congregation to whom they were originally preached; and in one or two of them ideas which I had found elsewhere are used and unacknowledged in a way which I should perhaps not have done, had I thought that the Sermons would have been published. I leave them, however, as preached, and simply express an earnest hope and prayer that the publication of the Sermons will, by the blessing of Him who is the God of all the families of the earth, lead those in and under authority to realize more and more the duties and responsibilities of their social standing.

E. B. T.

THE VICARAGE, ALNWICK,
Lent, 1872.

SINS OF THE FAMILY.

----•----

I.

THE HEADS OF THE FAMILY.

" Wives, submit yourselves unto your own husbands, as unto the Lord. For the husband is the head of the wife, even as Christ is the head of the church: and He is the saviour of the body. Therefore as the church is subject unto Christ, so let the wives be to their own husbands in every thing. Husbands, love your wives, even as Christ also loved the church, and gave Himself for it; that He might sanctify and cleanse it with the washing of water by the word, that He might present it to Himself a glorious church, not having spot, or wrinkle, or any such thing; but that it should be holy, and without blemish. So ought men to love their wives as their own bodies: he that loveth his wife loveth himself. For no man ever yet hated his own flesh; but nourisheth and cherisheth it, even as the Lord the church: For we are members of His body, of His flesh, and of His bones. For this cause shall a man leave his father and mother, and shall be joined unto his wife, and they two shall be one flesh. This is a great mystery: but I speak concerning Christ and the church. Nevertheless, let every one of you in particular so love his wife even as himself; and the wife see that she reverence her husband."
EPHESIANS V. 22-33.

ON the Sunday evenings during Lent last year, your attention was directed to an examination of the *Sins of Christ's Church.* But we must remember that the family is, as it were, the Church in miniature, and that there are *Sins of the Family,* of which we should be conscious, and which we should seek to remedy. May God bless to us the consideration of these during this season, so that whatever place in the family we may occupy, we may seek pardon for the past, and grace to exhibit greater faithfulness in the time to come. We must remember that the *family* is the most ancient relationship. And whilst appreciating the order of God in the Church, we must not forget the order which existed long prior in the family.

The first man whom God made in His own image was designed to be the father of the whole human race, or, at any rate, of the Adamic race. The first social relations which God constituted were those of the household. The only worship which we read of for 2000 years; beyond individual offerings, was family worship. Every tent had its altar; every patriarch was a kind of priest over his own house, presenting sacrifice for himself and his sons day by day continually. Until after the exodus, there is no token of any worship on a large scale; and even then, when God was about to do a new thing, and build His Tabernacle for a nation, the first ordinance which He gave in preparation for it, was an essentially *family ordinance*, the Passover, — " a lamb for a house."

There is something sacred in the family, which cannot on any account be dispensed with, for in it there is a distinct witness for God which cannot be supplied elsewhere.

True, the time had come when the family could no longer stand alone, when another and a grander polity, in which all the family of Israel are united, was to lift its more imposing front in the sight of the nations, when the families were to be gathered together and form a Church, as individuals gathered form the family; yet, even then, the former must not merge and melt away. The first step towards the new erection is another household bond and tie, a fresh fence set around the original and primitive enclosure. Its own peculiar sanctity must remain for ever inviolate.

Thus God's people have been ever taught —

and would that the lesson had been learnt !—that as the family is composed of the aggregate of individuals, so the Church is composed of the aggregate of families. The two must be kept distinct. God, as in other things, so in this, whilst leading up to higher standings, conserves the past. The family exists still; and so far, and so far only, as the duties of the family are performed faithfully, will there be a blessing upon the Church composed of those families ; "and no faithfulness in the Church (it has been most truly said) can compensate for neglect in the family. Ecclesiastical relationships cannot be built upon the ruin of households." In the family, then, as in the Church, there are those who are to obey, and those who are to be obeyed ; and that family is disorderly, as that Church is lacking in order, where those in authority do not exercise that authority which is theirs, or where those under authority are lacking in deference and obedience.

The necessity of order, and not confusion, is evident, when St Paul, writing to the Colossians, joins together "your order and the steadfastness of your faith in Christ," and says that he rejoices as he beholds it. In the material creation, what utter ruin would ensue if one of the heavenly bodies ceased to maintain its own position, and moved out of its appointed orbit ; can it be less in the spiritual creation ?

I need therefore say nothing as to the great importance of the social subjects which I have promised to bring before you during this season. May God open our eyes, that we may in our families exhibit more of God's order, and that were an apostle to visit us, he too might joy in beholding "your order, and the steadfastness of your faith in Christ." I shall have to speak plainly on many things ; but whilst they will be faithful words, may God make them loving words ! " Faithful are the

wounds of a friend,"—" The ear that heareth the
reproof of life abideth among the wise ;" and I
would speak the truth in love, "that ye may grow
up unto Him in all things which is the Head, even
Christ." Notice, ere considering the various duties
and relationships in detail, the connection with what
has gone before. The former part of the epistle
has been occupied with a description of the mystery
of Christ, which had never been made known in
other ages, but was now revealed by the Spirit to
the apostles and prophets of the New Dispensation.
This mystery was, "that the Gentiles should be
fellow-heirs, and of the same body, and partakers
of His promises in Christ by the Gospel." The
result of the declaration of this mystery was "to the
intent that now unto the principalities and powers
in heavenly places, might be known by the Church,
the manifold wisdom of God." Thus the Church
was to exhibit, even to angels, God's wisdom. " I
therefore, a prisoner of the Lord, beseech you," &c.,
iv. 1-3. Chapter iv. then presents us with the order
in the Church—an order from which we have griev-
ously departed ; and therefore the saints are not
being perfected, the body of Christ not being edi-
fied. From Chapter iv. 17–v. 21, are given general
Christian duties, closing with " submitting yourselves one to another," &c., and then, from v. 22–
vi. 9, are special directions to different members of
a family, expanding, in their case, the idea of submission in the fear of God. Thus, the fulfilment
on our part of our family duties is a proof that we
have understood the wisdom of God and His eternal purpose. It is also even more than this. " Be
filled with the Spirit." How ? "Speaking to yourselves in psalms and hymns and spiritual songs,
singing and making melody in your hearts to the
Lord ; giving thanks always for all things unto
God and the Father in the name of our Lord Jesus

Christ ; submitting yourselves one to another in the fear of God." Therefore, if we lack submission —if our houses are disorderly—we have not the Spirit ; and "if any man have not the Spirit of Christ, he is none of His." Oh, brethren, if this is so, can we remain content any longer with our homes and families in disorder ! Let us this Lent listen to Him who says, " Set thine house in order."

The apostle naturally commences with the husband and wife, and therefore we do also. And it is but fit ; for if *they* do not fulfil their mission, if their work is faulty as regards themselves, there will be failure in the whole household. They have to be patterns and ensamples. And therefore it is, that when the husband and wife are lacking in order, the children and the servants will lack also. I can only, in these sermons, give an outline for your thoughts and meditation. It would be impossible to exhaust any one of our subjects, even if the whole of Lent were given up to that alone. To-night, then, I would address myself to *the Heads of Families ;* and in so doing, we shall have to review the true relationship which the husband and wife bear to one another. Such a subject is most necessary in these days. Even our Parliaments have done much, and are doing still more, to separate that which God hath joined together. The *divorce courts* witness to many a fearful domestic scene, of which it is a shame to speak, and disclose unfaithfulness which is a scandal to Christianity. The license given to marriage being performed in a *Registrar's office*—solemnised it is not ; it is a solemn farce—has tended, in our large towns especially, to degrade the divine institution of marriage ; and a member of Parliament intends, I believe, to bring forward a Bill to legalise marriages for a term of years—two, three, five, or more years ; that the two are to enter into partnership, as it were, viewing marriage as a civil contract only. I am not surprised at it, and in course of time it will doubtless pass. It is only a fair and logical conclusion from what has been already done to throw down the barriers which surround the holy estate of matrimony.

Instituted in the time of man's innocency, we see what God's purpose in it is; and though neglected, misunderstood, and desecrated by heathen and Jew, it is restored in the Church of Christ—a restitution, however, from which the natural man recoils. Yet prosperity and blessing are bound up in it.

What is the Christian idea of marriage, and of the relation which exists, so long as both remain on the earth, between husband and wife?

"The husband is the head of the wife, even as Christ is the Head of the Church." On this the whole is based; and therefore to know our duties to those with whom God has united us, is to be able to work out in daily practice this simple rule of three—

As Christ is to the Church, so is the husband to the wife; and

As the Church is to Christ, so is the wife to the husband.

The relation of Christ to the Church is that which exists between husband and wife—Christ is the *Head* of the Church. He loves the Church, and nourishes and cherishes it. When His Church came into existence, between her and Him was formed a bond more holy, tender, and firm, than any that had yet been formed between God and man. "We are members of His body, of His flesh, and of His bones." And they who are in like manner joined

together by the Lord, have laid upon them the
duty of representing upon earth the image of this
union between Christ and His Church. Hence
the words, " Those whom God hath joined together,
let no man put asunder." Yet can we be surprised
at the lax way in which the marriage betrothal is
regarded, when we remember that that which it
represents is disregarded by the mass of Christendom ? Alas! yet so it is ; there is a divorce between Christ and His Church, so far as men's faith
is concerned, and this must lead to the other.
How little do we grasp this fact ? By baptism I
am one with Christ ; as a member of His Church
I have been betrothed to Him, and He to me.
He has taken me " for richer, for poorer, for better,
for worse." Yet we have been brought up in the
idea that we have nothing to do with Christ till
our conversion, and that that, not our baptism, is
the starting-point of our union with Christ. We
have been unfaithful to Him, yet He has never
cast us off. He still pleads, " Return unto Me, for
I am married unto you."

Now, if this were but believed by us, should we
not be more forbearing when there is provocation
given by one or other ? " How much have I been
forgiven by the Head of the Church ? shall I be
less forbearing to him or her to whom I am married ? " Yet this is, especially by the working-
classes, utterly forgotten. Again and again we
hear in our visiting the sad tale of a deserted wife,
or of a wife who has deserted her husband—why ?
Because he is a bad husband—drinks, makes home
so wretched. Oh! if one such hears me to-night,
think again : Christ, the Head of the Church, has
never deserted you, in spite of your sins and trans-
gressions. In the Gospel our Lord plainly declares
the oneness of the married, and St Paul repeats it
(Mark x. 11, 12). And even in the case of adultery,

it is a question if sanction be given to divorce or re-
marriage.

And the cause of failure is, because marriage is
now officially regarded as a mere civil act, and that
the Church's act is unnecessary, and that the blessing of God may be despised. Even if the law of
the land allows it, no Christian should avail himself
of it. If desirous of fulfilling the peculiar duties
of Christian marriage, it is only the marriage which
is blessed in the Church which is furnished with
the blessing needful to Christian life in that state.
Otherwise he must draw down upon his whole
life that gloomy shadow and indelible reproach of
denying and failing to fulfil his Christian calling.
The Christian may only enter into marriage with
a perception of its highest aim, and with an acceptance of its highest sanction and blessing.

Husbands, *love* your wives. It is not sentiment,
but love. The world's love decreases, for it is only
sentiment. The Christian's love has only begun ;
it grows daily stronger and stronger, and ever pre-
serves its freshness. Christ's love to His Church is
undying ; therefore the Christian husband's must be
the same.

The object which Christ has is the sanctification
and cleansing of the Church. Thus, too, should the
husband seek and aim at the sanctification of his
wife, remembering that she is "the weaker vessel,"
and that they are "heirs together of the grace of
life." Not only should he lead her in Christian life
and conversation, but do all he can to make the full
blessing of God accessible to her in the Church ;
and ever, at home, sustain her in spirit, strengthen
her in seeking after heavenly things, and forward
her in Christian knowledge. He is responsible for
it. The head of a congregation will have to give
an account of those to whom he ministers ; the head
of a family will have to do the same with those

entrusted to him—entrusted to him as a holy thing; not only must he preserve, but confirm and perfect his wife—he is appointed to bless her. How concerned, then, should we be about the preservation and increase of the spiritual life in those whom God has given us to love and cherish. Yet is it so, when so many women, as soon as married, or as soon as their families spring up, forsake the house of God, and all ordinances of religion? Many a time have I been told by a mother, that she used regularly to come to church *till* she married, and then years have elapsed, and she has never been, except at the christening of a child. The husband may himself go—but she, never! Is this recollecting that you are "heirs together of the grace of life?" Is this carrying out the representation of Christ's Headship? Does He care thus so little for us?

Then, for the duties of the wife : " As the Church is subject unto Christ, so let the wives be to their own husbands, in *every thing*." " Wives, subject yourselves unto your own husbands, as unto the Lord." " Submit...... as it is fit, in the Lord." And why this full and faithful obedience? " That if any obey not the Word, they also may, without the Word, be won by the conversation of the wives, while they behold your chaste conversation, coupled with fear."

Now, this cuts at the very root of one of the most deadly doctrines of the present day. Women are, so some say, to be regarded as men. " Rights of Women" is the cry, and all distinction between man and woman is to be disregarded. Ah! they wrong women, *Christian* women, who would thus establish the rights of women.

True, in the Christian sense, they are one—namely, in their relation to God as His Church, in communion with Christ, in enjoyment of the Holy Ghost, in all connected with spiritual things ; but whilst this is so, the subordinate position of woman, established by God at the creation, remains un-altered. It is confirmed, not upset, by Christianity, and to acknowledge it is a fundamental principle, if harmony is to be secured ; yet attempts are being made to set it at defiance. God's rule is being thrown off ; the rule of the husband is also disregarded ; the authority of Government, either in Church or State, the authority of parents, the authority of the husband, can alone be preserved in its sacredness and as a blessing, so long as the authority and rule of God is a reality accepted and acted upon. Man may misuse his authority, and cause it to be despised ; but the one who honours it, even in spite of misuse, honours God, and will be honoured by God.

To try to disentangle the knot apart from, and contrary to God, will bring a curse, and no blessing.

But the rule is not to be a despotic one : Christ's rule in the Church is not thus. There is in His government the tenderest gentleness on His part, and yet reverence on her part.

The power to rule is not to be considered but as a duty—a right which involves responsibility of the deepest and most solemn kind. In vain can he plead that he has not exercised the reins of govern-ment from love of peace, and to hinder domestic discord. Gently and wisely, but yet firmly, he should ever exercise that power which has been placed in his hands—not by man—but by God.

Remember, too, that all government is for the blessing of the governed—" Govern them, and lift them up for ever." Authority, therefore, must not be roughly seized, else it will depress, and not lift up and exalt those under authority. He is to rule therefore, to be the support, not the tyrant, of all who are his.

She may and must remonstrate, if she sees that

the course he proposes is objectionable ; but when she has thus spoken, let her call upon God to guide his will aright. The wife's advice is thus honoured and valued, but yet the decision must be his, not hers. Sarah obeyed Abraham, calling him lord, yet he was commanded by God to listen to and fulfil her wish.

She is his help-meet, and each should look upon each other in this sacred light.

How is it to be, where the husband is worldly, careless, ungodly ? Still the marriage relationship exists, and must be kept. In the time when the Epistles were written, there were many Christian wives with heathen husbands, yet, " Be in subjection," that " if any obey not the Word, they may without the Word be won by the conversation of the wives." The duty towards one another is therefore unaltered, even by the worthlessness of moral character ; the fulfilment has become immensely more difficult, but the duty is not lessened, but all the greater, and to her piety will be granted an especial grace and strength to fulfil it.

In honouring him she honours Christ, who has set him to be her head. And the pure conversation and life of a patient, loving, hoping, obedient wife, will win the heart of any one, even without and apart from the Word. It is not by asserting her superiority, or by crying down her husband's sin, that she will gain him to the Lord, but by patiently and prayerfully fulfilling her mission to him " in the Lord."

Family worship is essential to this. The praying together of husband and wife must and will ever be a great safeguard against all setting aside of this relationship ; and as prayer is an acknowledgment of our dependence upon God, it is a daily confession that our respective duties towards one another can only be fulfilled by help from God, through

Him who is the Head of the Church.   How many art there in this congregation who thus kneel together?   Of this, however, I will speak more in the concluding sermon, and I will not therefore dwell on it now.

Brethren, I do pray that in all things you who are placed as heads of families may thus regard one another "in the Lord."   Out of Him you can do nothing ; but Christian husbands and Christian wives may be assured that "His grace is sufficient, that His strength is made perfect in weakness."   Ask Him ever for it, and let your prayer, as you kneel together, and as you kneel alone, be, that you may by your love, regard, and considering and helping one of the other, show forth to an ungodly world that you are representing that undying love which exists between Christ and His Church, which nothing can annul.   Let the husbands govern, and thus lift up and exalt their own wives.   Let the wives be governed, and thus be blessed.   Journey together through this life, heirs together of the grace of life ; and when the Bridegroom cometh, you will enter with Him, and sit down at the marriage supper of the Lamb.

II.

CHILDREN AGAINST PARENTS.

" Children, obey your parents in the Lord : for this is right. Honour thy father and mother ; which is the first commandment with promise ; that it may be well with thee, and thou mayest live long on the earth."

EPHESIANS vi. 1-3.

LAST Sunday we glanced rapidly at the position which heads of families hold with respect to one another ; that the husband is designed to be the head of the wife, and is therefore to guide, direct, bless, and sanctify the wife, and that the wife is to reverence and obey, and to be a help-meet for her husband ; that the conduct of each towards the other is to be learnt by a consideration of the behaviour of Christ towards His Church, and that which she should shew to Him.

How does Christ act towards His Church? so and so only should the husband treat his wife. How is the Church expected to behave towards Christ, her ascended Head? so should the wife be to her husband. Earthly relationships are the shadow, the image of heavenly. Christ is the Church's husband, and it is because of this relationship that they who are by marriage permitted to reflect it, should imitate Him, and shew like conduct.

I will go further, and say that no real blessing, in its full and highest sense, can attend that Christian who does not seek to exhibit this truth. The husband and wife who lose sight of the spiritual truth which they are called to illustrate ; the parents and child who, in their intercourse with, and conduct

B

towards, one another, forget that they are the representatives of their Father in heaven, whose children we all are ; the master and servants who are unmindful that they both have a Master in heaven, must fail of reaping the full blessing which God would give them if they fulfilled their respective duties with a view to His glory. We may see this the more clearly by bearing in mind why the Church is, in Holy Scripture, always symbolized in prophetical writings by the " moon," and Christ by the " sun."

The moon has no light of her own, only what she derives from the sun, and which she reflects. The glory of the moon is when " full," *i.e.*, when the sun shines upon the hemisphere without any earthly impediment ; the quarters and phases of the moon are by the earth eclipsing the light, and intercepting it on its way from the sun to the moon. So it is that the glory of the action of the Church, or of any individual member, is only full when the Divine rays from the Sun of Righteousness fall and light it up, unhindered by anything which is of the earth earthly. May we ourselves be sensible of this important truth, and let it influence our conduct, whatever be our station in life.

To-night we consider, in due order, that which the apostle has adopted, " *The Sins of Children towards Parents.*" May the younger members of our congregation take heed, ere it be too late ; and though we reserve till next Sunday the sins of parents to children, I would ask you to examine your own selves, and see whether, if your sons and daughters do make themselves vile, and are disobedient, the blame does not lie very much at your own door.

" Children, obey your parents in the Lord : for this is right. Honour thy father and mother; which is the first commandment with promise; that it may be well with thee, and thou mayest live long on the earth," v. 1–3. So, Col. iii. 20, " Children, obey your parents in all things ; for this is well-pleasing unto the Lord."

How does St Paul, writing under the influence of the Holy Ghost, speak of the last days : " This know also, that in the last days perilous times shall come, for men shall be . . . disobedient to parents, unthankful, . . . without natural affection." How exactly does this describe these days, when all gratitude for the past is allowed to be unrequited, and it is considered unmanly to submit to "every ordinance of man for the Lord's sake," and to honour our parents.

Children *obey* your parents ; *honour* them.

If we refer to the Duty to our Neighbour, where the Fifth Commandment is expanded, we find this : " To love, honour, and succour, . . . to submit my-self, . . . to order myself lowly and reverently."

Headship must be understood. The wife must understand that the husband is to govern and to lift her up. If she attempts to assume the *rule*, disorder must take place. So with the children. The children are not to rule, but to be ruled ; not to govern, but to be governed. They are to be lifted up ; they cannot lift themselves.

The *father* alone has authority ; and the mother, as the father's help-meet, is to be obeyed, and to exercise authority, since she shares it from her oneness with her husband. They have it direct from the Lord ; therefore it may not be presumed upon ; therefore they may not use it as they please ; therefore they are accountable for the right exercise of it.

As with husband and wife, so with father and children ; rule is meant to be the ministration of blessing ; love must be the essence of it, and its life. It is willing and loving obedience which we are to cultivate and draw out from our children, and nothing will beget such obedience if authority be not blended with love.

We must *love* our parents, therefore, if we would honour, succour, and obey them ; love is the *spring* whence all the rest *flows*.

How are we to *obey* and *honour* them ?

By fulfilling their *commands*, and by cheerfully complying with their *wishes*. Not only must we do what they tell us, but we must do what we know they would wish. If we really love a person, we are not always waiting to be *told* ere we do a thing—a *wish* is enough ; and even if a wish is not implied, yet if we know that something would please that one, how cheerfully shall we do it ! Who is there on earth that has such right to a child's love as a parent, a father and mother ? Surely their slightest wish should be done, however indirectly it be expressed, and even if not expressed, yet if known.

Now, perhaps few children will be wilfully disobedient, will intentionally set at defiance what their parents tell them ; but it is often this, that the obedience is given with such bad grace, that it is altogether spoiled. Who can call that obedience, where the face, bright and smiling a few seconds ago, is now clouded over, the lips pouting, the brow contracted, even if the act enjoined be performed ? No ; it must be loving obedience, cheerful obedience, else it is not worthy of the name. That which expresses " I must, or I shall be punished," is a paltry kind of obedience. " It is my duty and my privilege—my highest honour." This is what is pleasing to the Lord.

But what children do often forget is this, that the known wish must be obeyed no less than the direct command. Children must not be casuists, and they have no right to draw a line between a parent's wish and a parent's command. " Our

Father—Thy *will* be done." So with our earthly
parents, who represent and shew forth our Father
in heaven. Yet how seldom is this done! A
child is asked by another one to go somewhere,
or to do something. That child knows full well
that his father and mother would not like him
to do it, yet he excuses himself by saying, "They
have not *told* me *not* to do so ; I am not therefore disobeying them." The young man keeps
company with, and makes a companion and a
friend of, one with whom he knows his parents
would never wish he should associate ; yet he has
never been forbidden, and so he thinks it is not
disobedience ; and often sin and misery is the
result of this secret and unavowed friendship, but
yet one which has been persisted in. The friendship is sometimes with a young woman ; and how
often is shame and disgrace the result of this conduct ! Oh ! never be ashamed of saying boldly,
"I know my father, were he to know it, would not
like it. My mother, I am sure, would not be
pleased; and I must regard their wish no less than
their word. Their will is my law."

Again, we are to honour them, not only by our
obedience, but by our *respectful behaviour.* How
many a child and young person is wanting in this
respect! There is more than one family which I
could name where the younger members never
address their father except by "Sir," and if they are
seated when a parent enters, always rise. This has
been enjoined, even from the earliest times (Lev.
xix.). We have the Fourth Commandment, and
then, "Thou shalt rise up before the hoary head, and
honour the face of an old man, and fear thy God : I
am the Lord." Respectful demeanour in their
presence, respectful language when speaking of
them to others — not needlessly exposing their
failures, not receiving slightingly their reproof, if

not actually resenting it : all this should be ex-hibited.

There is yet a further duty : love, honour, and *succour*. They have helped us when we were help-less ; in turn they become dependent on us, and we are not to cast them off. " Despise not thy mother when she is old." And so St Paul, in directing what widows are to be placed on the church list, thus describes them : Those whose children or grand-children act piously towards them, to whom is ren-dered the honour which God commands ; and the children are to requite their parents for their care of them. Yet if a son has to help towards the support of his parents, as far as his means allow, is it not often spoken of as a hardship and a burden ?

How does God's Word abound with beautiful examples of filial obedience : Isaac with Abraham, Jacob with both his parents, Joseph's deference to his aged father, Moses with his father-in-law, Ruth with her mother-in-law, Solomon in the grandeur of royalty paying respect to his mother, the Rechabites hearkening to the command of their father, even though dead ; and last of all, He who "suffered for us, leaving us an example that ye should follow His steps," in His own dying agony bade the disciple whom He loved tenderly to care for His own beloved mother.

" Children, obey your parents *in all things*." I would have you mark this : no exception—" *in all things*." There are, alas ! parents who lead their children into sin ; there are commands to obey which would not be to obey " *in the Lord;*" but to expect such things should never enter into a child's mind. And where he has reason to fear such things, he must arm himself, not with intention of rebellion, but with trust in God, that He will not let matters come to such an extremity. The command is everlasting : " Honour thy father and thy mother."

" Children, obey your parents in the Lord : for this is right." He will, if it comes in contradiction with another and higher command of obedience to God, make a way to escape from it. The child or young person must call upon God to preserve him from the sad necessity of refusing his obedience. His guidance will lead us through every difficulty. Faith in a living God is for ever our resource and strength in every time of need. God is the founder, He is also the sustainer, of all parental authority ; and as we saw last Sunday, the prayerful but obedient wife will be heard by God, and answered and blessed in and for her obedience to an unbelieving husband ; so will the prayerful and obedient child be blessed for his obedience.

A word to *mothers*. On you, to a very large extent, depends the obedience and honour of your children. They will see whether you obey your husband in all things ; and if you fail, what can be expected but that they should ? Then again, you must uphold your husband's authority. You heard this morning the sad story of a whole family sinning (Gen. xxvii. ; note vers. 6–11). Here was the mother directly bidding her son to defeat her husband's wishes. Could such conduct be really blessed ? How bitterly was Jacob himself deceived by his own sons ! And Rebekah also had her share of suffering. Her son had to leave home, and she never saw him again. There the disobedient child is sure to be where the mother refuses her proper obedience to the father, where his arrangements are despised, and his commands made of none effect. The authority of one parent can never be undermined by the other, without the authority of that one being weakened also.

God's blessings ever come from above. He is *above*, and therefore the course of blessings always flows downwards. The family blessings come from

parents to children. They are the instruments
through which the preserving power of God works
on those under them. The relation between the
two main pipes must not be discordant, else the
flow of blessing will be checked.

"Joying and beholding your *order*." I said last
Sunday ταξις meant the military order and discipline of a regiment. But what is this ? There are
colonels of regiments, captains of companies, with
their subordinate officers, and the privates. The
colonel's orders are given, and the men of each
company are told what to do by the captain :
they do not tell the captain. So with us ; and
Christian order in families is only to be obtained
by each one fulfilling his duties towards others as
in the sight of God.

Let me specially urge upon all children and
young people to shew this sacred obedience to
those who are over them in the Lord. In due
course, on Sunday morning fortnight, we shall
again speak of the Fifth Commandment, and it
will then be shewn how that the commandment
requires not only "to love, honour, and succour
thy father and mother," but also "to honour and
obey the Queen, and all that are put in authority
over you." All authority—parental, social, ecclesiastical, or political—is to be regarded. Democracy
is the ruin of every government, however fair the
outside may be. The people ruling in the Church
is equally fatal to any church order and government ; and not less disastrous are the conse-
quences when children and young people refuse
the parental control and subjection. To-night we
cannot go into the wider field. It is the parental
authority which I would now uphold.

Society has done much to throw down this barrier. You constantly find lads, and young men and
women, paying their father and mother so much of

their wages in order to keep them. Among manu-
facturing and colliery populations this is the regular
mode, and more or less in other places. Such a
thing should never be allowed. The wages of all
should be handed over, to make one common fund,
and any allowance made by parents to their children considered as a gift, not as a right. The evil of
the other system is at once seen. The person who
pays his parent so much for his board and lodging
is placing himself in no other position than a mere
lodger. He is renouncing the headship of his
father, and so we constantly hear, " I pay so much ;
if you are not satisfied, I shall leave and set up for
myself." And many a mother acknowledges that
she can do nothing with her children as soon as
they begin to earn wages for themselves. All this
must be wrong. What any of the family bring in
is not their own, but for the common good of those
with whom they live. And those families are far
happier where there is one common fund. I men-
tion this, because I am convinced that the social
and political independence of the young tends very
much to promote that *religious independence,* and
breaking away from all control, which is the curse
of Christendom, especially among the families of
our labouring classes.

But remember that even if society does not
expose you to this snare and temptation, as a
Christian you are bound to fight against and overcome it. Remember it is not manly, neither is
it Christian, to despise authority. Manliness,
Christianity, is to be able to abide in that state of
life in which God has placed us, and *in it* to
do God's will. Oh ! love, honour, and obey your
parents. They deserve every regard for what care
they have taken. Never resist their authority ;
never speak evil or lightly of them. They represent to you the fatherly love of God. In obeying

them you obey God ; dishonour them, and you dishonour God. Your conduct to them is to be the same as your conduct to God ; He is your Father, and the father in the flesh is His earthly representative. The viceroy must be regarded as the Sovereign himself. What they do to you is because of the place in which God has put them. They may fail : the representative authority may very imperfectly shew the true authority ; but for any failure on their part they will have to answer to God. Your path is clear and distinct : "Honour thy father and thy mother." "Children, obey your parents in all things ;" obey them "in the Lord." Your strength lies in this ; for "in the Lord have I righteousness and strength." "Go in this thy might ; have not I sent thee ?" Yes, your might is because God has commanded you, and He will help you to keep His commandment. Pray for your parents, and let it be believing prayer, that they may be taught to rule in the Lord ; but He who has called you to be a son or daughter will enable you to obey those who are over you, and thus to do the thing that pleaseth God. Don't take the reins in your own hands. Don't seek to exercise an authority for which you have no grace given you. Let your motto be, Duties are ours, results are God's, and His Word ever is sure. " Them that honour Me, I will honour ;" and most true it is. " He that receiveth you, receiveth Me ; and he that despiseth you, despiseth Me."

PARENTS AGAINST CHILDREN.

" And, ye fathers, provoke not your children to wrath : but bring them up in the nurture and admonition of the Lord."

EPHESIANS vi. 4.

LAST Sunday we spoke of that unswerving and unhesitating obedience in the Lord which Christian children are to render in all cases to their parents, and that the authority of the parent should be regarded as the outward exhibition of the authority and rule of the Lord, Whose representative and viceroy in the family he is.

I suggested then that the absence of order in the family, the lack of obedience to their fathers and mothers, is not altogether to be laid at the door of the children, but that the fathers and mothers had very much to blame themselves for in the disorder of their children. Has there not been a provoking spirit on the part of the father ?—has there been an endeavour that the children should be brought up in the nurture and admonition of the Lord ? And thus, by failure of government, the children have been discouraged, and not lifted up and exalted.

I am sure of this, that the blame should be much more taken home by parents. We find that it is so in other relationships ; why not in this ? Take the case of a nation. We all know how nations rise and fall, how God lifteth one and setteth down another. We have seen it most terribly illustrated in that war which has been raging for some months past between two of the great powers of Europe,

which is for a while, at any rate, suspended.   That
it will be a permanent peace few, if any, can imagine ; and though no nation has a right to say, that
because she has been successful, therefore she
is the favoured of God ; and, similarly, no nation
because unfortunate in the issues of war, should be
condemned as an exceeding sinner, for the humbling
of a nation may be blessed by God far more than a
nation lifted up by pride and success ; yet still we
know that the misfortunes of a country are always
attributed to the mismanagement of the government.   To a great extent this is undoubtedly true,
and in the case of families it is still more so.   The
ruin and disorderly condition of a household may
be traced very much to the misgovernment of the
heads.   They have somehow failed, and hence
anarchy and internal rebellion have necessarily followed.   It is this subject, the failure of domestic
government, the sins of parents towards their children, which is our subject this evening.   I want you
to believe this truth,—" Train up a child in the way
he should go, and when he is old he will not depart
from it."   There is no limit to this promise.   And
if the child does depart, it *must* be because some
important element of education has been omitted.
Some disproportion of one part or other has hindered the efficiency of the whole.   Abraham, training up his family for God, finds Him faithful that
promised.   Eli and David, good men but bad
parents, have to learn, by bitter experience, God's
" breach of promise."

   The whole system of Christian education is con-
tained in these few words—" Bring them up in the
nurture and admonition of the Lord."

   " Nurture" and " admonition" must be distinguished from one another—the former is rather
the discipline, the correction which is needful ; the
latter is a milder term, it is the monition which is

taken home and laid to heart. And it must be
"of the Lord," such as He would sanction and
approve of and bless.

Let us glance, then, at the whole process of education, and throw out a few hints in connection
with it.

Education begins from the hour of the child's
baptism, and that fact should give colour to the
whole course of education. That this is so, may
be seen from the fact, that the Hebrew word
translated "train up" in Proverbs, is, in Deute-
ronomy xx. 5, and elsewhere, used to convey the
idea of dedication ; so dedication of Solomon's
temple (1 Kings viii. 63). Now, the baptism of
a child is in Scotland called "the dedication."
The training, therefore, is the dedication of a new
house to God, fitted for His service and use ; the
heart made meet for God's indwelling. And this
fact, accomplished and indelible, should ever hold
an important place. Every act, even the act of
repentance and return to God, must be founded
upon the consciousness that God has made us His
children ; and there is no motive like this for
moving us to seek Him with heartfelt repentance,
if we have even in the least degree departed from
Him. How can we, then, expect that God will
acknowledge an education which begins by mis-
taking, denying, and wiping out from the consciousness of the child what God has already done
with him ? It is the high privilege of the Christian
child that from the first he may regard himself as
the child of God, and can look up to Him as
"Abba, Father." Baptism is no empty formality
—no merely human action, but a Divine act, by
which we receive a spiritual life from union with
Christ. This life may be quenched, it may be
injured by neglect. It is with this higher life of
the regenerate as with the natural life of the new-

born babe; it is tender, and requires unceasing care. And so far from making the child pre-
sume, and sin because he is an object of grace,
rather from the consciousness of his Christian
standing, and from grace received in baptism,
arises the deepest penitence and sorrow for sin,
the strongest desire to imitate the holy child Jesus;
and yet, while sorry, he will not be crushed or
discouraged, because he knows how much he is
beloved of God. Let a parent forget this, and
what harm and loss is incurred! They are heirs of
a heavenly kingdom who are placed under your
charge, that they may be preserved for their calling in Christ Jesus, and prepared to enter into the
enjoyment of it when Christ comes again. And if
we know the value of a jewel lent to us, how
watchful shall we be so as to preserve it! This,
then, must never be lost sight of; never forget
yourself, never let them forget, that they have been
received into the family of God, and, as "dear
children," should strive to be like their Father in
heaven. Let their views of God be those of affection, of love, of reverence, never those of terror or
of fear. What child is afraid of a father? Yet,
how painful is it to hear the language of some
parents respecting God.

The child grows in years, and by degrees habits
of truth, of purity, of faith, are inculcated. Obedience is instilled. They are taught by command,
and then, as they grow older, the reason why. We are
not to reason first, but to have faith, and to reason
after on that in which we have faith. Truth must
be instilled in children from the very beginning.
The world, as opposed to Christ, is one huge lie,
and your children have to be taught how to walk
through it unharmed. How can they do this if you
are not true yourselves? Without your truthfulness nothing can be made of theirs. But how often

is this forgotten? A promise is made, but never performed; a threat uttered, but never fulfilled. Oh, let your children ever depend on what you say. Be truthful to them, even in the most trifling things, and upon this their truthfulness will develop itself.

Then, as to *faith*. All around we find mistrust, and doubt, and scepticism. There is no faith in the powers that be, none in holy things, none in ordinances. Teach them to have faith in God. Let confidence be felt by them. Let them be assured that God is true in all His acts, in all His ministries, in all His ordinances. Shew that you have faith, and they will learn it. Yet parents often do the reverse; they send their children to church and to school, but don't come themselves. They teach their children some form of prayer, but never pray themselves; they themselves act as if there were no God; how can their children believe that He is?

Then, as to *purity*. Believe me, what I said on this subject on Sunday was not in the least expressed too strongly. I believe that what I said has offended some; but truth must be spoken, especially on these subjects. The purity of your children must be an unceasing object of care and anxiety. All around is impure, and fleshly sins abound, as do falsehood and unbelief. Immodesty must scare away the Holy Ghost, the Spirit of purity, and everything should be done by which the purity of your children may be preserved. To foster this threefold spirit is, then, the object and aim of all education rightly so called; and if the parent in any way hinders the truth, the faith, the purity, he is committing as great a sin as he can against his children.

"*Train* them *up*." The consecration to God begun must be continued, the spiritual house must be dedicated and indwelt in.

But the simile expressed in the word *train-*

ing implies still more. The young plant must not only have an upward growth, but it must be kept within bounds. As the plant grows it must be fastened by fresh bonds, which will support it, and keep it from trailing on the ground. How pitiable the sight of any creeper which has been allowed to grow unrestrained, and, instead of being beautiful, is spoiled and injured, and defiled by dirt. So it is that children, like plants, need careful training. The crooked and gnarled old oak cannot be bent straight; but the young oak can, by proper management, be so helped at first, that it will continue. And so God's Word is sure, and parents should believe it, and be confident of success, if they do their part. "Train up a child in the way which he should go, and when he is old he will not depart from it." "Bring them up in the nurture and admonition of the Lord."

The "nurture and admonition" represent respectively the sterner measures which may be necessary in childhood, and the monition which is taken home and laid to heart.

Nurture. This same word is rendered "chastening" in Heb. xii. and elsewhere (Heb. xii. 5-10). The end, therefore, of this "nurture" is to hold down in death the old man which has been put to death by God. The suckers must be ever guarded against, but they are ever coming up again. And similarly in the baptized; the old man has only been put to death, and laid at our feet in such a manner, that we, if we are unbelievers, can call it back again into life, and can yield to sin a fresh dominion over us, which will be harder and heavier than before. "The last state of that man shall be worse than the first." That which Christ has with bitter sufferings overcome and put to death, we should not again bring up from the grave ; but we are so weak that we must be watchful, and exercise discipline.

And all discipline should be such as to remind us of the fatherly purpose to save, to purify, and to heal. Therefore, " a rod is for the back of him that is void of understanding." " He that spareth the rod hateth his son ; but he that loveth him chasteneth him betimes." " Withhold not correction from the child ; for if thou beatest him with the rod he shall not die : thou shalt beat him with the rod, and shalt deliver his soul from death."

Yet, whilst God's Word strictly enjoins this stern discipline, and one which is absolutely necessary if the spiritual life of the child is to be preserved,—if he is to be saved from eternal death,—remember, however, that it is to be " the nurture *of the Lord.*" Our Heavenly Father never lifts the rod if the gentle voice of admonition will prevail. Continued finding fault is most injurious. Correction is medicine, not food—the remedy of occasional diseases, not the daily regimen. The storm may deepen the roots, but will never produce fruit. This is done by the warm sun, genial showers, and nightly dew. How many parents fail in this respect, and so sin against their children !

They never lift them up ; they even discourage them. Incessant fault-finding ; never a word of praise or encouragement. Oh ! how unlike this is to the fatherly correction of Christ (compare the epistles to the seven Churches) ; and then disgust, hatred, and rebellion are sown.

The " nurture of the Lord " aims at another sin. How many parents threaten, but withhold the rod ! It is only used as a threat. Our Father in heaven —His threatenings are not vain words. If His children will not turn, He will whet His sword, He hath bent His bow. The firmness of truthful discipline can alone convey a wholesome influence. " Lord, do Thou be pleased to strike in with every stroke, that the rod of correction may be a rod of

C

instruction !" The nurture of the Lord does not even stop here. His discipline is severe as often as we need it, and His visitations come upon us, not so as to be least painful, but so as most surely to root out and slay the will of the flesh. And yet He does it in moderation ; it is never excessive, never more than really necessary. He doth not afflict willingly ; and as soon as He sees that we bow down and acknowledge our faults, " He healeth the broken in heart," and quickens us again with His consolations, so that we may know His love even in His correction.

Combined with nurture is admonition. The word of reproof which sinks into the heart : this is the meaning of the original. It is more than mere *remonstrance.* Eli said to his sons, "Nay, my sons, for it is no good report that I hear ;" yet it is expressly said of him that " he restrained them not "—he " admonished them not" (same word). The reproof must be therefore such as will be felt, and which must be acknowledged.

St Paul gives still further advice : " Provoke not your children to wrath." " Provoke not your children, lest they be discouraged."

In all needful nurture and admonition, the parent should bear in mind that "the wrath of man worketh not the righteousness of God." In every sin which a child commits there is much need of humility on the part of a parent. Let there be no anger in it and after it ; and where penitence is shewn, let there be no repetition of reproaches, no continual reminding of the past. It is this incessant raking up of old sins that disheartens and estranges a child ; and if once he is embittered by harsh recollections, and his heart closed, who can tell the result ? In all, let it be felt that punishment is not an angry impulse, but a high necessity ; and when he is humbled, and knows the misery of disobedience, then let him see and feel the fulness of your love. 'Tis thus the Lord acts to His penitents, and in the renewed enjoyment of your love he will be comforted. After the storm the seed finds the soil warmed and softened. The hour immediately succeeding a punishment is of the most vital importance.

Parents shrink from correction, or else carry it to an undue extent. The discipline of the Lord should ever be borne in mind, and He has left us an example that we should follow His steps. Let all needful discipline be used in dependence upon God. Let all teaching be given, as to the Divine nature in the child, in similar dependence. Be conscious yourself of the jewel lent you ; let your child be conscious also, and you will both do all you can to return the same to God who gave it. Be yourselves what you would wish them to be. " Example is far better than precept." Remember that on the proper training depends the temporal welfare of the child. What if *untrained*—what if *badly trained?* A broken leg badly set is even worse than unset. And this will encourage you. Be kind and loving to them ; rejoice in their little joys ; weep with them in their little troubles ; let there be confidence and loving trust, and the needful discipline, when had recourse to, will never be resented, but submitted to, and in the end there will be gratitude. How many parents only use their parental authority to find fault ! There cannot be love, there can be no real home in that case ; and it should be the unceasing aim of a father and mother to make the home of the child the seat of all his happiness, and of all pleasant recollections ; yet how many, from this having been neglected, and the bitterness without any of the sweetness being only known, never care to revisit the home they have left.

Oh ! that I could persuade parents who are here to-night, thus to ponder the deep responsibility before God which, having children, is laid upon you, and to seek to discharge your duty with unceasing prayer for special grace and wisdom. Oh ! what wisdom is needed to guide, to repress, to bring forth, develop, and improve the hearts and wills of your children ! The rebellion of Korah, the sin of Achan, the neglect of Eli, the wickedness of Jeroboam and Ahab, the perverseness of the rebuilder of Jericho, caused trouble to their houses. Oh ! the irregularity of a head, the neglect of your responsibility, has made many, and will ever make them, to inherit the wind.

Let integrity, as before God, be the broad stamp of our family relations. Let God's Word be our rule, His ways our path. And even if you may never see it—if death calls you hence before the Lord come, and *after* you, having served your own generation by the will of God, shall have fallen asleep, yet, in the day of Christ, when all things shall be revealed, the children's blessing shall be found in the Book of Life, linked with the prayerful exercise of the parents' faith and love.

" Lo, children are an heritage of the Lord : and the fruit of the womb is His reward. As arrows are in the hand of a mighty man ; so are children of the youth. Happy is the man that hath his quiver full of them : they shall not be ashamed, but they shall speak with the enemies in the gate."

These arrows are placed in the hand of every parent. You have the direction of them. Let the aim be true, and the string drawn with sufficient force, and, all counteracting influences overcome, the arrow will hit the centre, and the mark of the prize of our high calling will be obtained.

Are any convinced of sin and failure ? Do you feel that you have been unfaithful to God in the exercise of that authority ? Oh ! remember that "if any man sin, we have an Advocate with the Father, Jesus Christ the righteous." "If we confess our sins, He is faithful and just to forgive us our sins, and to cleanse us from all unrighteousness." For all family sins there is the blood of the Lamb, and "when I see the blood, I will pass over it." I shall have to speak of this in our concluding sermon ; but I would remind you now and ever that He waiteth to be gracious — to help and to strengthen. He is the God of all the families of the earth, the Father of all His children. You, therefore, who are to shew Him forth, may look to Him for help, and be assured that "the blood of Jesus Christ His Son cleanseth us from all sin." Go this night and confess to Him your shortcomings as parents. He heareth the cry of the penitent, and will abundantly pardon.

If, as we have seen, husbands and wives are to reflect in conduct Christ and His Church, so, let me assure you, your children must see in you the glory of God—"the God of all the families of the earth." Pray over, watch over your children, as heirs of a heavenly inheritance. Say yourself, and teach them to say, not with the empty language of the lips, but with the grateful expression of the heart, "Behold, what manner of love the Father hath bestowed on us, that we should be called the sons of God : Therefore the world knoweth us not, because it knew Him not. Beloved, now are we the sons of God, and it doth not yet appear what we shall be : but we know that, when He shall appear, we shall be like Him ; for we shall see Him as He is. And every man that hath this hope in him purifieth himself, even as He is pure."

IV.

SERVANTS AGAINST MASTERS.

"Servants, be obedient to them that are your masters according to the flesh, with fear and trembling, in singleness of your heart, as unto Christ; Not with eye-service, as men-pleasers; but as the servants of Christ, doing the will of God from the heart; with good will doing service, as to the Lord, and not to men: Knowing that whatsoever good thing any man doeth, the same shall he receive of the Lord, whether he be bond or free."—EPHESIANS vi. 5-8.

WE have hitherto spoken of those natural relationships which exist in the family. To-night we have to speak of the social relationships. Husbands and wives, parents and children, have hitherto been our subject, and their respective duties to one another. To-night we have to deal with masters and servants; and, still preserving the order of the apostle, we have to consider the sins which *servants* commit against their *masters*.

Our text enumerates various duties: Obedience—good-will; not eye-service. In Colossians, "Do it heartily, ye serve the Lord Christ." See also 1 Tim. vi. 1, 2—"Let as many servants as are under the yoke count their own masters worthy of all honour, that the name of God and His doctrine be not blasphemed. And they that have believing masters, let them not despise them, because they are brethren; but rather do them service, because they are faithful and beloved, partakers of the benefit. These things teach and exhort." Titus ii. 9, 10—"Exhort servants to be obedient unto their own masters, and to please them well in all things; not answering again; not purloining, but shewing all good fidelity; that they may adorn the

doctrine of God our Saviour in all things ;" and in
1 Pet. ii. 18–21—" Servants, be subject to your
masters with all fear ; not only to the good and
gentle, but also to the froward. For this is thank-
worthy, if a man for conscience toward God endure
grief, suffering wrongfully. For what glory is it, if,
when ye be buffeted for your faults, ye shall take it
patiently ? but if, when ye do well, and suffer for it,
ye take it patiently, this is acceptable with God.
For even hereunto were ye called : because Christ
also suffered for us, leaving us an example, that ye
should follow His steps."

From a consideration of these passages we shall
have plenty of material. But before entering into
any detailed examination, a few words on service
in general, as influenced by Christianity.

Servants, at the time of Christ's coming in the
flesh, were not in the position they now occupy, but
were *slaves*, and as such were exposed to ill-treat-
ment and to hard usage, which no one would now
give to a servant. Yet it is worthy of notice, that
Christianity interfered very little with the institutions of society. It was not because there was not
much which required to be changed, for the social
system was very ill arranged ; Christianity would,
indeed, where its principles were introduced and
thoroughly carried out, act upon the politics as well
as the morals of the land, but yet made it no part
of its business to excite prejudice by any appearance
of an endeavour to " turn the world upside down."
Christianity came with one message—" Repent ye,
for the kingdom of heaven is at hand ;" and this
equally applied to king as to peasant, for all had
sinned. It would, when received, set right and
reform that in which one had sinned against another,
but it did not require this reformation previous to
its own reception. Not only was it not destructive,
it was eminently conservative and constructive ;

not only did it abstain from interfering with much opposed to its spirit, but even supported existing institutions by requiring of its disciples that they should be content, whatever their condition. The slave is not taught to seek for freedom. If he had his choice he might choose; but let every man abide in the same calling wherein called, and in that calling seek to adorn the doctrine of Christ, doing his duty in that state of life in which it hath pleased God to call him. How thoroughly does this contradict and reprove the teaching of many reformers in the present day, and who shew by their language how little of the mind of Christ they possess!

Christianity is most vehemently opposed to all those levelling theories which disaffected men and women so industriously circulate. True, all are one in Christ Jesus—all have the same grace, the same sacraments, the same faith, the same hope of glory. But, nevertheless, Christianity is the best upholder of the distinctions of society; and that man has read his Bible to very little purpose who does not see in it God's appointment, that there should be, in His world, rich and poor, master and servant; that want of loyalty is want of religion; and that there is no more direct rebellion against the Creator than resistance to any constituted authority, even though that authority may err; or the endeavour to bring about that boasted equality, in which all shall have the same rights; or rather—is it not?—in which none shall have any. The French cry of 1789, " Liberté, Egalité, Fraternité," is the cry, not of Christ, but of Antichrist. " Order is heaven's first law." There are ranks and degrees among the holy angels of God; there must be ranks and degrees on earth. And the humble cottager, with his wife and family in a single room, living by the use of the spade and plough; the artisan, who from Monday morning till Saturday afternoon pursues the same dull routine ; and the servant, whose days are consumed in the drudgeries of the kitchen or the stable, as well as those in the higher ranks of life, trade, or business, or engaged in other professions, are all taught by Christ to serve God where they are, and that in their secular engagements they are to serve Christ.

Thus with servants, the class about whom we are speaking specially to-night. In performing the duties of their position,—as others in doing their allotted work,—they are doing service to Christ. Every lawful employment, rightly discharged, may be considered as discharged in the service of the Saviour, and your labour is not in vain in the Lord, and the Lord will reward you.

" Ye serve the Lord Christ." Oh ! domestic servants, or any who are under authority and employed by others, your masters according to the flesh, regard yourselves, each one, as servants of the Lord, and that every occupation is assigned to you by Him who is your Master.

In the Church, which is the household of God, there is one grand difference between His servants and those of an earthly lord and master. Take that of an earthly sovereign, or of any great person. However different the occupations of the various members of the household, all are under one master ; and the duties which the lowest servant has to perform, are such that the master has a direct interest in their discharge. With many such earthly masters, who have large establishments, some of the servants may be but little known. The upper servants are those who have most contact with the master, and through these the under servants receive their directions. But the beautiful thing in the service of Christ is, that the eye of the Master is as much on one servant as on another ; His acquaintance with one as actual as another, and that each one is, as it were, known unto Him. In all things he serves the Lord Christ. Worldly employments, therefore, however menial, do not withdraw you from the service of Christ. All are necessary to fill up the body of Christ.

Now, if servants would but act on this principle, doing all things as to the Lord, how different would be the conduct of many! He, and he only, acts as to the Lord who does his work most conscientiously and most honourably. The common mode of acting is to act only as to men, as though only having to do with men ; and hence all those deeds which are utterly inconsistent with this—" Ye serve the Lord Christ."

Is it not forgetting this, that not only is there so much complaint now about the difficulty of getting good servants, but also of getting servants at all ? Young women now do not care about going into service. They aspire to something better, where there is less control and more independence. But is this Christianity? Why should any station be despicable where Christ may be as actually served as by the highest in the realm ? It is Christ who has placed you where you are— Christ who has given you your work to do. The merest drudge, then—and we shall speak next Sunday (*D.V.*) of the disgraceful way in which many masters and mistresses make their servants drudges—but even so, the merest drudge may be cheered, and her spirits brightened by this : God, Whose I am, and Whom I serve. And then, too, think of Him who said, " I came not to be ministered unto, but to minister." " I came not to do Mine own will, but the will of the Father that sent Me." He was a servant—" Behold My Servant." Surely it is an honour to occupy that position which our Lord and Saviour did ! He served, and now is "the Master ;" and by learning yourselves

to " serve," you will be best following His example,
and be fitting for the Master's coming, when it will
be said to all who have faithfully served the Lord
Christ, "Well done, good and faithful servant,
enter thou into the joy of thy Lord!"

The "few words" have become expanded beyond what I had intended, but not, I trust, unne-
cessarily, or without the hope of some good. For
unless servants will bear in mind that they are " the
servants of Christ," it is utterly impossible for them
to carry out the apostolic directions with respect to
their conduct towards masters. But as the wife is
to see in the husband the representative of Christ,
the Head of the Church, and is therefore to love,
honour, and obey him, not only for his own sake,
but for the Lord's sake, Whose Headship he represents ; as the child is to see in the parents the representatives of Christ, and God the Father of all
the families of the earth, and especially the Father
of all the baptized, and is therefore to obey,
please, and respect them, submitting to their discipline, hearkening to their admonition, not only
because they are his parents, and for their sake,
but so as to please Him whose Fatherhood they
represent, and for the Lord's sake ; so are servants
to see in their master, not a mere man to whom
they have engaged themselves, and in whose service
they live, and for which they expect a return in
pounds, shillings, and pence, but one whom they are
to serve truly, ever bearing in mind,·that in serving
him they "serve the Lord Christ."

"Ye serve the Lord Christ." If you do this, the
following will be easily admitted, and you will
gladly avoid all which, being a sin against your
Master Christ, is also a sin against your master
according to the flesh.

"*Be obedient,*" ver. 5. (See also Col. iii. 22.)
"Servants, obey in all things your masters." There

may be—I fear there are too many—masters who often bid their servants to do things contrary to God's law. In these cases have recourse to Him, your Master in heaven, and ask Him to dispose and govern the heart of your earthly master, that he too may remember that he has a Master in heaven. Still, in all cases, it would be well for a servant to suspect his own judgment, backward in asserting what he considers, or even knows to be his rights. But in most matters the servant should bear with many things, rather than resist authority.

But just as children may obey, but so unwillingly, and with such sulky looks and pouting lips, that the obedience is worth nothing, so, St Paul says, not only "obey," but "with good will," and "do it heartily." Take pleasure in what you do, for remember that you are serving Christ. Yet this is often not done ; and specially so with the servants of the middle class families. It is very often the fault of the masters and mistresses, but yet the personal character of your employer should not affect the cheerful and hearty compliance with any wish or command. Whilst in his service, you are bound, because you serve Christ, to obey your master diligently and pleasantly, cheerfully and respectfully.

Then, St Paul says in his Epistle to Titus, "*Not answering again.*" Oh! how do servants sin by forgetting this! There are many servants who make a point of always answering again, disputing the propriety of almost every command ; if reproved, answering again with a retort and bad language. It is incumbent upon all, especially those under authority, to bear with any harsh treatment, not answering again, or adding fuel to the fire—not rendering railing for railing.

Again—not with *eye-service.* I fear that there

are very many eye-servants in employment,—
whether it be out-door or in-door work. How
common is it to put on an appearance of activity
and diligence when the master's eye is upon them,
and seem then to be hard at work ; but let the
back be turned, and immediately they are idle.
Yet "eye-service" is enjoined ; only, let it be the
consciousness, that though your master may be
absent, yet you have a Master in heaven, Whose
eye is unceasingly upon you. Your time belongs
to him who pays you for it ; and therefore, if you
are idle or waste your time, you are robbing your
employer. When sent on an errand there should
be no dawdling. You have work to do—do it, and
remember that you are ever accountable to God.
At the Mint, where all our gold and silver money is
coined, a man sits, unseen by all, though seeing all
himself. He can watch the actions of each one engaged on the premises, but is so situated himself
that he cannot be seen by them. So is it with our
Master. Nothing we do, whether good or evil, can
escape His all-seeing eye. He sees all, though we
cannot see Him.

Faithful service requires that there should be *no
purloining*, *i.e.*, making away with what belongs to
your master. Most servants have many articles
within their reach, which may be taken, and never
discovered ; yet it is a *sin*. And this, whether you
take it for yourself or give it to others. You may
be considered good-natured and generous, but it is
an act of gross dishonesty, and betrays a trust
reposed in you. Let this be your rule, never to
take, never to give away, what you know you would
not take or give away if your master were looking
on. Yet this is often violated, and especially in
large families ; the cooks and others give away bones
and scraps of meat, bread, and sundry things, which
they have no right to do. There are so-called

perquisites, which are recognised as yours ; but what is over and beyond these, you should never regard or consider as belonging to you.

Faithfulness in little things is necessary if you would be faithful in great things, and the most scrupulous honesty should be shewn with regard to all those things which are placed in your hands or in your charge ; and pilferings and petty thefts are equally *sins* against your master as if you committed a wholesale robbery.

Again, "shewing all good fidelity," desirous in every way of promoting his master's welfare, and that of the family. Yet this is not done, when you hear something said at the dinner-table, repeat it among your fellow-servants, reveal it then to others, and idly talk with people who may come to the house about your master's affairs. If you are to act with all fidelity, it must not only be with regard to your master's property, but his honour and his secrets.

And thus act, not only to the good and gentle, but also to the froward ; and it is remarkable, that it is in connection with this commandment to servants that St Peter says, that which we all know so well : " Christ also suffered for us, leaving us an example, that we should follow His steps" (1 Pet. ii. 18–25). The example of Christ, therefore, is one which is especially suited for servants to follow. It is not pleasant to be blamed and found fault with for what we have not done ; but take it patiently ; " it is acceptable to God, hereunto were ye called." It is therefore God's appointment ; He knows it, and He will, if you are faithful, reward you. See Christ even in those who act least like Christ, and do service as to the Lord, and not as unto men ; and count your master worthy of all honour, that the name of God and His doctrine be not blasphemed.

There is another matter which, if unnoticed altogether, would leave our subject incomplete.

The happiness, well-being, and order of a family, not only depend on the parents and children acting rightly, but the children towards one another. An elder brother or sister exercising authority over one younger, commanding as none but a parent should, instead of exhorting and intreating as a brother, causes ruin in a family. So too, if servants act wrongly towards one another. Quarrels among servants are as prejudicial as differences between masters and servants. Members of the same household should cultivate peace and good-will. Let there be kindly feeling shewn one to another, helping one another, and assisting one another, where possible, in acts of kindness; seeking, above all, to influence them as to their spiritual welfare, and by your own consistent and pleasant Christianity, recommending your religion to them. Need I add one thing more? Where men and women servants are in the same house, you cannot be too guarded in your conduct towards one another. Thrown much as you are in one another's company, never allow yourselves in any lightness of behaviour; never use immodest language, foolish talking, or jesting. Many a life has been made sad by such being encouraged.

"Ye serve the Lord Christ." In your conduct towards your master, in that towards your fellow-servants, be what you know Christ, your Master in heaven, would have you be. He sees all. He knows all. Never do what will displease Him.

The religious duties of the servant must not be omitted. As you have a Master in heaven, He is entitled in the first place to your thoughts and affections. You may not have much time in the day to yourself, but let it be a rule which knows

no exception, that you will daily read a portion of
God's Word ; that you will never rise in the morning, or go to bed at night, without praying to your
Master in heaven, to Him who is also your God
and Father.   Use the means of grace, and especially the Holy Communion, as helps to the faithful
discharge of your duties as to God.   I know there
is a great feeling among servants against liking to
be thought too religious.   Men-servants especially
are kept away from being communicants for this
reason.   Oh! if any such, and who are cowards
in this matter, are here to-night, remember " ye
serve the Lord Christ ;" and are you serving Him
truly when you neglect this command, " Do this in
remembrance of Me ?"   I am glad that many of
the servants in this congregation are communicants, but more should be ; and many of those who
do come, should come oftener.   Some are absent
because they do not like to speak to their masters
about it ; some, alas! because their masters do not
try and arrange so that they can come.   But somehow you should agree, that monthly at any rate
you should have an opportunity of obeying your
Heavenly Master's command.   This ordinance is
" for the strengthening and refreshing of your
souls ;" and placed as you are in a family where
the bond of union is but very slight, and with
fellow-servants, perhaps, who have but little, if any,
religion, your life is one of peculiar temptation,
and one, therefore, which needs peculiar grace, and
special recourse to every help whereby spiritual
life may be strengthened.

  " Ye serve the Lord Christ."   " I serve," let this
be your motto ; and when your day of service is
over, and your Master comes, may you hear the
welcome—" Well done, good and faithful servant,
enter thou into the joy of thy Lord !"

V.

MASTERS AGAINST SERVANTS.

" And, ye masters, do the same things unto them, forbearing threaten-
ing: knowing that your Master also is in heaven; neither is
there respect of persons with Him."—EPHESIANS vi. 9.

IT is a well-known fact, that in any failure of duty
there is generally fault on both sides. If children
are disobedient and unruly, parents may always
take the matter to heart, and blame themselves for
it. If wives are not rendering to their own husbands
that love, and obedience and reverence, which they
should, even as the Church does to Christ, the husbands may look to themselves, and see whether
their conduct is such as to secure this behaviour;
and so, if servants are not what they should be, and
often fail in being faithful servants, let the master
and mistress examine themselves, as to whether
they have acted rightly towards their servants. For
though God's grace alone can make us regard the
office, rather than the person of a superior, and
render to the froward the same obedience as to the
gentle and good, still, those in authority should take
care that by no act of theirs any stumbling-block
should be put in the way of others, and which will
make their obedience the more difficult. Hence
husbands should often see how they are acting
towards wives—parents towards children, masters
towards servants.

We spoke last Sunday of the sins of servants
against masters: to-night we have to glance at the
other side—those of *Masters against Servants.* And

the direction given is very short : "And, ye masters, do the same things unto them, forbearing threatening : knowing that your Master also is in heaven ; neither is there respect of persons with Him." And in Col. iv. 1,—"Masters, give unto your servants that which is just and equal, knowing that ye also have a Master in heaven." "Give that which is just and equal," and then they will be removed in great measure from the danger of purloining. Forbear threatening, and then they will have no reason to answer again. Render to them their due, and then they will give you yours. You are their master— their head. Let it be your aim to govern them, and "lift them up." You have a Master in heaven. Let this thought influence you in all your conduct towards those who, being also in the service of Christ, are really *your fellow-servants.*

Before examining these points of interest, let us glance for a while at Jewish laws regarding servants. We have the account of the way in which they are to be treated fully set forth in Ex. xxi. 1–6, and Lev. xxv. 39–55. In the year of Jubilee, every 50th year, all estates and conditions of the people were permitted to feel the hallowed and refreshing influence of this most noble institution. The exile returned, the captive was emancipated, the debtor set free ; each family opened its bosom to receive once more its long-lost members ; each inheritance received back its exiled owner. The sound of the trumpet was the welcome and soul-thrilling signal for the captive to escape, for the slave to cast away the chains of his bondage, for the man-slayer to return to his home, for the ruined and poverty-stricken to rise to the possession of their forfeited inheritance. No sooner had the trumpet's thrice-welcome sound fallen upon the ear, than the mighty tide of blessing rose majestically, and sent its refreshing undulations into the most remote corners of Jehovah's land. And it was immediately and intimately connected with the Day of Atonement. It was when the blood of the victim had been shed, and the High Priest had finished all his work within the veil, and had come forth, that the emancipating sound of his Jubilee trump was heard, re-echoing far and near, through every valley and over every hill in the land. Not a corner was to remain unvisited by the joyful sound. The basis of the Jubilee was as wide as that of the Atonement. To the special significance of this, we shall again refer. Let us now just glance at that part of it which shews the influence which the anticipation of it is to have upon the transactions between man and man. The scale of prices was to be regulated with reference to that day. If near at hand, the price was low ; if far off, it was high. All human compacts as to land were broken up the moment the trump was heard; for the land was Jehovah's, the people were all his tenants, and the Jubilee brought all back to its original condition. Whatever arrangements were made by the tenants themselves were therefore to be influenced by the nearness of this anniversary, and all was but temporary till restored by Jubilee.

We thus see the way in which servants were regarded. Only the heathen men were to be bond-servants. Their own poorer brethren were not thus to be engaged, but were to be considered as hired servants and sojourners till the day of jubilee, and not to be ruled over with rigour. " The poor shall never cease out of the land ;" and " The children of Israel are My servants, whom I brought forth out of the land of Egypt." These two thoughts are at the foundation of all true conduct towards servants.

I spoke last Sunday night of the necessity, the Divine appointment, of service, and that that one whose vocation is to be a servant of others, should still strive in all things to please "the Master;" in all things serving the Lord Christ, and looking for the reward when "the Master" returns. May I not add now that they are wrong who, under the fair and plausible cry of Freedom and Rights, shew an apparent zeal for the cause of the poor? The poor man's rights are demanded for him; political power is bestowed upon him; his wants are to be supplied by easy labour, and his feelings not wounded by overbearing masters. The apostles say not so; they teach not this doctrine. "Even hereunto were ye appointed." And yet more, "Christ died, leaving us an example, that ye should follow His steps," and the submission, cheerful and willing obedience, even to the froward and ungenial.

Observing travellers in countries where slavery still exists, tell us that the unbalanced and inordinate teaching of the truth of the common equality of all men, has had a most disturbing influence on their spirits, and excites them to discontent and revolt. St Paul and St Peter both shew that the introduction of the religion of Christ does not alter the relation between a master and a slave—it does not dissolve the tie; it brings grace to sanction and sustain it. Slavery was allowed by God under the Jewish dispensation; and yet I think that it is not too much to say, that the condition of a Hebrew slave was better than that of many a servant in a professedly Christian family.

Look again at what St Paul says to the Ephesians and Colossians: "Ye masters, do the same unto them, forbearing threatening;" "Masters, give unto your servants that which is just and equal: knowing that ye also have a Master in heaven." What is it that is the principle of these directions? Surely this, that the masters as well

as the servants should seek to realise the nobility
of service ; that there is a meaning in difference
of rank ; that the fulfilment of duty by any person
in any rank of life is to be respected and admired ;
and the master should remember that he who is
faithful in a low and humble position, would also,
with the same moral worth, have fulfilled the duties
of a less humble sphere, if such had fallen to his
lot.   Contempt, therefore, on the part of a master,
is utterly inconsistent with the teaching of Christ,
and the reaction is always fatal.   Treated harshly
because he is what he is, the servant seeks to repair
his honour by appearing something different from
what he is ; and by dress, as well as by other ways,
difference of rank is sought to be abolished.

"Just and equal," *i.e.*, that which they are by
agreement entitled to, and which in fairness they
deserve, even though not agreed upon.   How
many exact of their servants work for which no
arrangement was made, and for performance of
which no recompense is given ?   How many treat
their apprentice lads as if the object were to get
as much out of them as possible, and to pay as
little as possible, and require of them work of other
kind altogether to that for which they have been
apprenticed ?   This is not what is either just or
equal.   There is another way in which many
masters sin against their servants.   The Fourth
Commandment—a commandment which has been
binding on man ever since God rested on the
seventh day after creation—says, "The seventh
day is the sabbath of the Lord thy God ; in it
thou shalt do no work, thou, nor thy man-servant,
nor thy maid-servant."   And in Deut. v., where
Moses rehearses the Decalogue just before his
death, in the audience of all Israel, he thus spake :
"Keep the sabbath-day to sanctify it, as the Lord
thy God hath commanded thee.   Six days thou

shalt labour, and do all thy work : but the seventh day is the sabbath of the Lord thy God : in it thou shalt not do any work, thou, nor thy son, nor thy daughter, nor thy man-servant, nor thy maid-servant, nor thine ox, nor thine ass, nor any of thy cattle, nor the stranger that is within thy gates ; that thy man-servant and thy maid-servant may rest as well as thou. And remember that thou wast a servant in the land of Egypt, and that the Lord thy God brought thee out thence with a mighty hand and by a stretched out arm : therefore the Lord thy God commanded thee to keep the sabbath-day."

Are you thus caring about the spiritual welfare of your servants, and those whom you in any way employ ? Is it not that with many the servant is a mere drudge, upon whom all work is thrown, and who from morning till night has her bodily strength strained and exhausted to the uttermost ? We allow our beasts a day of rest. Do we allow our servants a day of rest from bodily work, so that it may be to them a day of worship and communion ? Is it not rather this, that we make it utterly impossible for our servants to come to the forenoon service ? "Well, but they get out in the evening." Yes ; but in the morning there is a service at which many, I know, of your servants would stay, did you make it convenient and enable them to do so. Many of those confirmed last year have been unable to stay for Holy Communion by the indifference or opposition of masters and mistresses. Religion is never meant to be in opposition to our duties. It is not serving God if we go to church and Holy Communion, and are neglecting our duties at home. But I am sure of this, that in every household it is quite possible for the mistress to arrange that her servants should come to morning service, and be able to receive the Holy Communion once a month at the least. And what is more, it is your duty so to do. Especially with younger servants, you are much in the place, and have the authority of parents towards them ; and therefore, in addition to doing all in your power to make them comfortable whilst in your service, you are bound by every Christian duty to watch over their spiritual welfare, and to strengthen them in the right use of all ordinances to which they have access.

Masters and Heads of Families! I do entreat you, in God's name, to think about this. Your conduct towards, and treatment of, your servants and those whom you employ, is a solemn subject of inquiry, and one which every Christian house-holder should consider. And the spiritual welfare of those thus associated with you, especially if young, is to a very great extent laid on you, and for which you will be held responsible. Not only are you to rest from your shops and your business on the Lord's day ; the day is also to be one of rest, so far as possible, and of spiritual joy, for your servants, that they " may rest as well as thou."

I referred last Sunday to the very loose idea that servants have as to the bond that should unite master and servant together—a mere ex-ternal matter, to be dissolved and changed at pleasure. How frequently do servants, on this account, change situations and go elsewhere for no reason whatever, and thus wander up and down, till at length they are dismissed in old age and sickness. The servant is much to blame, but are not masters much also at fault ? Have they done all they can to secure the attachment of the ser-vant ? Have they acted in such a way that the servant would be unwilling to leave and go else-where, because a few shillings or a pound extra in wages can be obtained ? How few servants remain now in modern families for eighteen, twenty, thirty years, as they did with our fathers and grandfathers? They are not to be blamed; it is the lack of interest and Christian feeling shewn by those in authority. The servant feels and knows that she is only kept for what can be got out of her. The higher relationship is not shewn by the master. Can we be surprised if the servant fails to shew it?

And now, what will put all things right, and help very considerably towards the true exhibition of a Christian and well-ordered family. The secret of Christian family life, and it is a secret worth knowing, and being acted out in spirit as well as letter, will be our subject next Sunday night. But, even to-night, we may learn much from what St Paul says—"Ye also have a Master in heaven." Yes, for high and low, for rich and poor, for master and servant, there is but one Church, one Word of God, one Sacrament, one Lord, one faith, one hope of our calling. In domestic life this unity must exist, and our equality before God must be shewn and acknowledged. You have a Master, and to Him you are held responsible. He is "the Lord." You are yourselves not masters, but servants; and those who serve you are fellow-servants with you of the same Lord. What then? "And the Lord said, Who then is that faithful and wise steward, whom his lord shall make ruler over his household, to give them their portion of meat in due season? Blessed is that servant, whom his lord when he cometh shall find so doing. Of a truth I say unto you, that he will make him ruler over all that he hath. But and if that servant say in his heart, My lord delayeth his coming; and shall begin to beat the men-servants and maidens, and to eat and drink, and to be drunken; the lord of that servant will come in a day when he looketh not for him, and at an hour when he is not aware, and will cut him in sunder, and will appoint him his portion with the unbelievers." And thus we revert again to the Jewish servant, and his release in the year of Jubilee.

Our year of Jubilee, our year of Release, will not be till the close of the Day of Atonement. Our High Priest is yet within the veil, pleading alone, in the very presence of God, the merits of His perfect Atonement—the Blood of the Lamb of God. The work of intercession still goes on, and we still wait without. But soon will the High Priest come forth, clad in His robes, and will bless the people who wait. And the trump of God, the Jubilee trump, will be heard ; the broken-hearted will be healed, the captive delivered, the bruised set at liberty, and the acceptable year of the Lord ushered in.

We have seen, that in the case of the Jew, all actions were regulated by the near approach or distance of the year of Jubilee. No one might exact or be harsh to another, because the year would soon be come, and all tenure of land, as all else, was only held till the year of Jubilee came round. Can we say the same? Do our great landowners, our merchants, our men of business, our tradespeople ; yes, do any of us live, referring all our actions to " that day ?" I fear not. Our thoughts are wholly set, for the most part, on the things of this day, and the approach of that day enters but little into our calculations ; yet, as the Jewish master regulated all his transactions, knowing that the year of Jubilee would upset the existing state of things, and make all revert to their original condition, and arranged accordingly ; so should we act with reference to the year of the Lord—the day when the trump of God will be sounded through the length and breadth of Christendom. And thus we should bear in mind, that the earth is still the Lord's. That this is so, a grand witness is ever borne into

the very heart of the money-making city of London,
where, above the portico of the Royal Exchange,
is inscribed, in letters which can be read by all—
" The earth is the Lord's, and the fulness thereof."
Whatever position, therefore, we occupy—the large
landed proprietor, it may be, with his thousands of
acres, it may be with his tens or hundreds ; the
small freeman, with his half acre ; the shopman, the
private gentleman, content with his own house—
we are all only but copyholders in reality in the
sight of God ; there is no freehold estate ; it must
all revert to Him when the Jubilee trumpet peals
forth. How then should we act ? We are not
owners, but only stewards. The heritage of our
fathers we may inherit, and, as faithful stewards,
we should seek to improve it—it is not our land, but
the Lord's ; we only hold it " till He come." Oh !
believe this, and shew it, by an earnest endeavour rightly to improve that which till then has
been entrusted to you, and yet sit loose to all
earthly position, because the year of Recompense—
the year of Jubilee—will come ere long.

Masters will only render that which is just and
equal, they will only be enabled to forbear threatening, so long as they remember that they have a
Master in heaven—a Master who will come again,
and who has placed us where we are, tenants-at-
will, saying—" Occupy till I come." They, on the
other hand, who deliberately say — " My Lord
delayeth His coming," they who forget altogether
that He will come, will usurp authority which is
not theirs, and will, through pride and forgetfulness
of God, abuse their position. Ask yourselves, therefore, this one question : Placed as I am in a position of trust, a master of others, yet I myself am
under authority, even the authority of Him Whose
agent and tenant I am, is this, is that which I am
doing, consistent with the truth, that I must give

back all to Him? Whatever is inconsistent with
the fact that the year of Jubilee is near at hand, is
a sin, not only against our fellow-creatures, but
against God, Whose servants we are bound to be,
Whom it should be our delight to serve faithfully,
and Who will, without respect of persons, judge and
reward every one according to his work.

We have thus glanced at the various social relationships—Husbands and Wives, Parents and Children, Masters and Servants. We have seen that all
are the shadows of spiritual relationships—God and
Christ and the Church. Forget the reality, and the
shadow must be imperfectly discerned. How then
may we best fulfil our respective duties, placed as
we each have been where we are by God—"The
God of all the families of the earth?" Let me again
remind you of an astronomical fact. The moon's
eclipse, and which hides her light, is by the earth
coming between her and the sun. All her light is
borrowed, reflected from the sun; and she is the
lesser light, meant to shed forth a measure of the
sun's light when he is hid from the earth, which is
buried in the shades of night, till the day dawn and
the sun arises. The new moon is when all light is
thus cut off. The various quarters and phases of
the moon are caused by a portion only being in
darkness. The full moon is when nothing obstructs
the sun's light, and then is she in her full glory.

So too with us; the Church of Christ, baptized
into one body, is the moon—the "Light of the
world," yet not shedding forth her own glory, but
reflecting Christ's. He is absent now, and "till the
day dawn and the shadows flee away," "till the
Sun of Righteousness arise," the moon, the Church
of the living God, is His witness. Why does her
light so often fade and grow dim? Is it not
because the world too often intervenes and inter-
cepts the light of Christ? Oh then, if we are to be

faithful husbands, wives, parents, children, masters, servants, we must watch and pray, and ever abide in the full and uninterrupted presence of Christ— then, and then only, shall we be able to shine upon a dark and sin-bound earth. " Let your light so shine before men that they may see your good works, and glorify your Father which is in heaven." We shall be able to shed some light, and then, when "the day" dawns, and "the Sun" arises, the light of the moon shall be as the light of the sun ; for we shall behold His glory, and share it with Him in the kingdom of His glory for ever and ever. Amen.

VI

THE SECRET OF CHRISTIAN FAMILY LIFE.

" Finally, my brethren, be strong in the Lord, and in the power of His might."—EPHESIANS vi. 10.

I DO not think that the Apostle means this section (10-20) to be separated from that portion which has been under our consideration. Both in this Epistle and in that to the Colossians, after closing his advice to those occupying the various stations in life, he proceeds to the same subject— "Be strong in the Lord, and in the power of His might," and this strength is here spoken of as watching and praying; so in Colossians, "Continue in prayer, and watch in the same with thanksgiving."

For we can only fulfil our duties as husbands and wives, parents and children, masters and servants, so long as we are watchful and prayerful. Both are necessary. We must watch and be on our guard. But "except the Lord keep the city, the watchman waketh but in vain." Therefore pray, put on the whole armour of God. Let us face every temptation, even though it be a giant. "I come to thee in the name of the Lord of hosts, the God of the armies of Israel, whom thou hast defied."

On these Sunday evenings, I am aware that I have been treading on dangerous ground. I felt it when I undertook these subjects, and as we have advanced I have been aware of it still more. Yet, are we always to avoid these dangers? Morality is

inseparable really from Christ's religion, and unless
our social and domestic and business relationships
are based on truly Christian principles, they must
sooner or later brake in two.   And it is because
the sins of the family are so flagrant, and the exhibition of a well ordered Christian family a sight so
rare, that I have given this subject such prominence.
The present age is one of revolution.   We see it in
France and Ireland at this very time.   It has
affected the lower grades of our own society to an
extent which few will believe ; and I have but little
doubt that the cause of the infection spreading is,
humanly speaking, because of the influx from these
countries, and the share they have in our work-
shops, manufactories, and mines.   Viewing the
matter from another range, I have equally as
little doubt that such a state of things is caused
by all Christendom having departed from the
ways of God ; the one Body, for the well-being of
which each member should labour and strive, is dis-
believed.   Each one thinks, each one cares, only for
himself.   The faults, I believe, are on both sides—
those in authority, those under authority.   " I am
as good as you."   The woman is equal to the man,
the child is as good as his father, the servant and
workman as much as his master ; and thus the whole
of society is turned upside down.   " Such things
ought not so to be."   You are Christians, and your
position in society should reflect and be the image
of your position as towards God.   And in deal-
ings with your fellow-creatures, you should ever be
the " full moon," and not let " the earth," and the
principles of the earth, hide and dim the light
which the Sun of Righteousness shines upon you.

To have a " full moon," there must be the clear
and uninterrupted light of the sun.   It is a natural
law, and part of God's order : if we are to be
brightly shining in the fulness of the reflected

glory of Jesus, there must be nothing come between us and Him ; no talk about expediency ; there must be contact with, and communion between us and Christ. Hence prayer.

Prayer is, however, of various kinds, each having its own peculiar significance. Public prayer and worship concern us as members of the Church of Christ, family prayer and worship as members of a Christian family, and private prayer and worship as individual members of Christ. None can be dispensed with. You may say your own prayers, but this will not excuse you from going to Church, or from praying with your family.

The secret of Christian family life is when all the three. are combined in proper proportions, no one surrendering its place to the other, and that family can only be well ordered and in fullest measure blessed of God, when every member engages in private prayer and worship, seeking for individual grace, and making individual confession ; where the whole family are gathered together morning and evening for family prayer and worship, commending the whole family to the care of the One Father, and seeking from Him pardon for family sins ; and also where every member of the family, husband, wife, children, servants—are regular in attendance on the ordinances of God's house.

Private prayer is, I hope, neglected by none of you. God knows, and you know yourselves ; I judge no man, and you come to the House of God, and join in the worship of the sanctuary ; but

Do you have Family Prayer ?

Morning by morning, and evening by evening, do you call your household together, and together praise the Lord ?

The common worship of the family is the oldest form of social worship. For 2000 years it existed before the worship of the Church. The father was the priest of the household altar. With the performance of this family worship God has bound up the prosperity of the Christian household. The obligation laid upon you, whether as husbands, wives, children, servants, remains the same, whether the family are collected together or not ; but the grace to fulfil these obligations can only be fully obtained where this duty is performed. God's name should be hallowed, and by God's Word, and by prayer, should our work by day, and our rest by night, be sanctified. Joyful thanksgiving in the morning, prayer for grace and protection in the evening, should be the subject. And remember that all should be present, as far as possible. Some read a chapter, and offer prayer with their wife and children, but the servants are never called in ; yet this is wrong, thoroughly wrong. If the common work of the day is begun and ended with our common recognition of our common Father, our common Master in heaven, it will be impossible for the master to fall into unnecessary reproach and threatenings. And it will have a similar wholesome effect on the servants. For the Spirit of Christ makes each one on whom He is shed abroad content with his place, and happy in filling it, and performing its duties to the glory of God. Each one, by this act, is confirmed in his own place, and the Christianity and dignity of those under authority being acknowledged by their joining in family worship, they will have a less temptation to resist authority. The master sows for his servants spiritual things, strengthening them in God, and they repay him by letting him reap of their carnal things.

Family worship, then, is a duty laid upon every

head of a family. Even in business it is often arranged that ere the day's work in the shop or business commences, there is a kneeling together of all connected, committing their ways to the Lord. In some of our large mills, the mill-owners regularly thus implore God's blessing ; the attendance is voluntary, but I have known some 600 or 700 come a quarter of an hour earlier, so as to join in reading Scripture, prayer and praise ; and in the first bazaar in London—the one in Soho Square, and now the largest of any of those in London—it is the regular practice, ere the business of the day begins, for all the stall-holders to join together in worship. And it is most remarkable the blessing to individuals who have thus begun the day with God.

I would help you, brethren, in this matter tonight, and will therefore shew you the duty, but also try and remove the difficulty which I know many feel in reference to it.

1*st.* "Is it not enough if we pray separately?" No; there are family *sins* which the family should confess ; there are family *wants* for which the family should jointly make supplication ; there are family *mercies* in which all share, and for which all should with one voice give thanks ; there are judgments and dangers in which all are concerned, and all should lend their help to prevent them—"A threefold cord is not quickly broken."

2*d.* Though assured of the propriety, still there are difficulties urged. "I cannot pray before others." How do you know it ? Have you ever tried ? You may expect God's help in the faithful performance of duty. "I am not eloquent, but slow of speech." Who makes the dumb to speak ? "Who hath made man's mouth ; have not I, the Lord ? Go, and I will be thy mouth, and will teach thee what thou shalt say." And remember, "the key opens not the

E

door because it is gilt, but because it is fitted to the
lock." God looks not at the gilded utterance, but
at the fitting word. "God be merciful to me, a
sinner ;" and use the same prayer daily if you will ;
it is but what the Church does in her public worship,
when daily the same prayers are sent up to the
throne of God. "God will never shut His child out
of doors because he comes not every day in a new-
fashioned suit." And if you do not like, or if you
feel yourself unable to give expression to your
desires before others, there are many manuals of
family prayer which you can use.

But is it really on this account that you neglect
family worship ? You who neglect God, and give
Him no place in your family, is it not that you give
Him little, if any, in your own secret chambers ?
If you really knew the joy of communion with God,
I cannot think you would rob your family of the
opportunity. If you had found the treasure yourself, you would not hide it from those of your own
flesh and bones. And how can you expect your
family to walk in the fear and love of God, if they
thus know Him not as their household God ? "It
is no wonder to see that tree thrives not, which
stands but little in the sun, and as little wonder
to see them continue profane and wicked, that
but once in the week come under the beams of an
ordinance."

There is another objection made. "So difficult
to get all together." Yet why should it be ? If
the family is well-ordered, surely at nine, or half-
past nine at night, all should be in-doors as a rule,
and then the chapter read and the prayer offered
before retiring to rest. There may be some difficulty in the morning, though, even then, I know
it can be managed, where there is a sense of need of
God's protecting grace, but in the evening there is
none ; and I am confident that you would find a

recompense, even in the *morality* of your families, as well as the nourishment of personal holiness, were the morning and evening thus honoured and sanctified by you.

I trust, however, that there are some families where the Name of God is called upon. To you a few words.

It is not enough to set up the worship of God in your house, and not enthrone God in your hearts. From the act, therefore, look to the end. You are but playing the hypocrite all the while, and God says—"Dost thou at all pray to Me?" Remember, then, not to blot and mar a holy duty by an unholy life. "If thou meanest to foul thy hands with sin's black work in the day, why dost thou wash them in the morning by prayer? It is to no purpose to begin with God, and to keep company with the devil all the day after. It is but a little while thou art seen upon thy knees, and a little seeming zeal at thy devotion will not gild over a day's sinful miscarriage." Christ preached with power and authority, not as the scribes. Why "not as the scribes?" They sat in Moses' chair, and were the authorized and recognized teachers of the land, but they had lost reverence by not walking consistently—they said, and did not. If you would have your family worship be with power and authority, be pure in life. Let there be harmony and peace in the family. How can you with one voice join in " Our Father," if you are contentious'? Prayers must be hindered by contentions. You know the poet Burns' description of the " Cottar's Saturday Night ;" let this be the scene in your family daily.

How to conduct Family Worship.

Obviously the head of the family is the divinely appointed priest of his own household, and the one

who therefore, confident in God who has called him
to occupy that position, should never delegate his
place to another. It enables the children and
servants to look to the father and mother as the
guardians, not only of their bodies, but of their
souls, and their earnest intercessor at the Throne
of Grace.

The daily reading of Scripture is essential to the
well-being of your family. Read the Bible through
from beginning to end. " All Scripture is given by
inspiration of God, and is profitable for doctrine, for
reproof, for correction, for instruction in righteousness ;" and the Lord has His message in every
chapter. Lead your children to search the Scrip-
tures. Read, mark, learn and inwardly digest them
—Deut. vi. 4-9. Then kneeling down and realizing
that you are in the presence of God " our Father,"
whether the language be your own, or the prayers
be composed by others, let the spirit of prayer be
cultivated. Be specific. Family wants, sins, fail-
ings, mercies, your neighbours' families, the families
which make up your congregation, " all the families
of the earth."

One caution : Don't be long, so as to try the
attention of young children, or be tedious to your
servants, especially when in the evening they are
tired with the day's work. Be earnest whilst engaged, and let it be the savour of the remainder
of the day, and only hereafter will the full blessing
be known.

Family prayer, it has been truly said, " keeps
alive a genial interest in one another's welfare—it
speaks continually for God and to God ; it keeps
heavenly things before the mind, and corrects the
deadening contact with the world ; it brings constant supplies of Scripture truth before the family,
and then gives a heavenly cast to their thoughts,
opinions, sentiments, as they are growing up to

riper years ; it keeps God always before them ; it
conciliates His merciful regard, it sweetens every
cup, it forms a habit of prayer, and teaches the fear
of the Lord ; it draws off your household from trifles
and shadows, and accustoms them to the reality
of life, and preparation for the deeper realities of
eternity ; it suspends their converse with men, and
teaches them the greatest of all lessons, that man's
business and man's happiness, whether in youth or
age, trial or prosperity, in time or in eternity, as
master or servant, is to converse with God through
Christ Jesus, that he may be changed into the
same image from glory to glory, even as by the
Spirit of the Lord."

It is said of David, that after a hard day's work,
when the ark was brought back which had been so
long without a home, and the first steps taken for
providing a magnificent temple, which his son
built : " Then David returned to bless his house."
He puts forward no hint of fatigue. He had been
engaged in Divine service all the day ; he had been
singing and dancing before the Lord with all his
might ; the anxiety of arrangement had fallen on
him alone ; the psalms they sung were his ; it was
he who had presented the burnt-offerings and
peace-offerings ; it was he who had blessed the
congregation ; and now what he had done upon
so grand a scale, he repeats in miniature—he returns to bless his house. Can we with this pattern
before us excuse ourselves ?

And this same King David is an example, too,
that family worship alone is not enough, when the
life is inconsistent. A few chapters further on,
and we have placed on record the matter of Uriah,
which brought ruin in the family. Family worship
and family blessing are not enough, unless the example of family holiness is exhibited also.

And now we close our consideration of the Sins

of the Family. God grant that, knowing His will, we may seek for grace to fulfil it. The close of any course of teaching is always solemn. We cannot be the same, now that Lent is closed, as we were at the beginning. We know our duties now better than we did. The reason of different relationships has been set before you ; you have perhaps never thought of it before. Lent must leave you altered either for good or evil. God grant that, if sadder, you may at least be wiser, and remember for your help—" The blood of Jesus Christ His Son cleanseth us from all sin"—" He that spared not His own Son, but delivered Him up for us all, shall He not with Him also freely give us all things ?" Let this week be a week of sitting at the Cross of Christ. " Sitting down they watched Him there." Contemplate the agony and bloody sweat, the cross and passion, the precious death and burial, and then on Easter rise with Christ, on the day of His glorious Resurrection, to newness of life. I would beseech you to keep holy the anniversary of Christ's death. Oh ! who can spend in merriment and enjoyment that day when even the heavens mourned : " Darkness over all the earth !" " O come and mourn a while ;" it was your sins that crucified Him, for you that He died.

And as to family prayer, you could not have a better time than this very night to commence, if family prayer has been as yet unknown ; to recommence it, if the habit has been given up. You have to register your household this night. A form for this purpose has been left in the house of every person throughout Great Britain. I have spoken on the subject this morning, seeking to turn your thoughts to another census — the Census of Heaven's kingdom. As you fill up the forms, and ask the questions which are necessary from those residing with you, bend your knees in prayer with your assembled household—thank God " our Father " for the mercies of the past ten years, for the many blessings, temporal and spiritual ; thank Him for the daily proofs of love, for any increase and growth in grace ; and setting down the names of one and another, oh ! let it be the utterance of your hearts, " Make them to be the numbered with Thy saints in glory everlasting." Let this be the burden of your prayer and thanksgiving this night, and having once done so, never let a day begin or end without kneeling down with your household and praying to our Father in heaven.

Oh ! listen to Jeremiah's cry—" Pour out Thy fury upon the heathen that know Thee not, and upon the families that call not on Thy name," and look forward to that day of which Isaiah speaks— " And it shall come to pass, that he that is left in Zion, and he that remaineth in Jerusalem, shall be called holy, even every one that is written among the living in Jerusalem : when the Lord shall have washed away the filth of the daughters of Zion, and shall have purged the blood of Jerusalem from the midst thereof by the spirit of judgment, and by the spirit of burning. And the Lord will create upon every dwelling-place of Mount Zion, and upon her assemblies, a cloud and smoke by day, and the shining of a flaming fire by night : for upon all the glory shall be a defence. And there shall be a tabernacle for a shadow in the daytime from the heat, and for a place of refuge, and for a covert from storm and from rain." Is. iv. 3-6.

Commercial Printing Company, Edinburgh.

Ingram Content Group UK Ltd.
Milton Keynes UK
UKHW021356250423
420747UK00007B/435